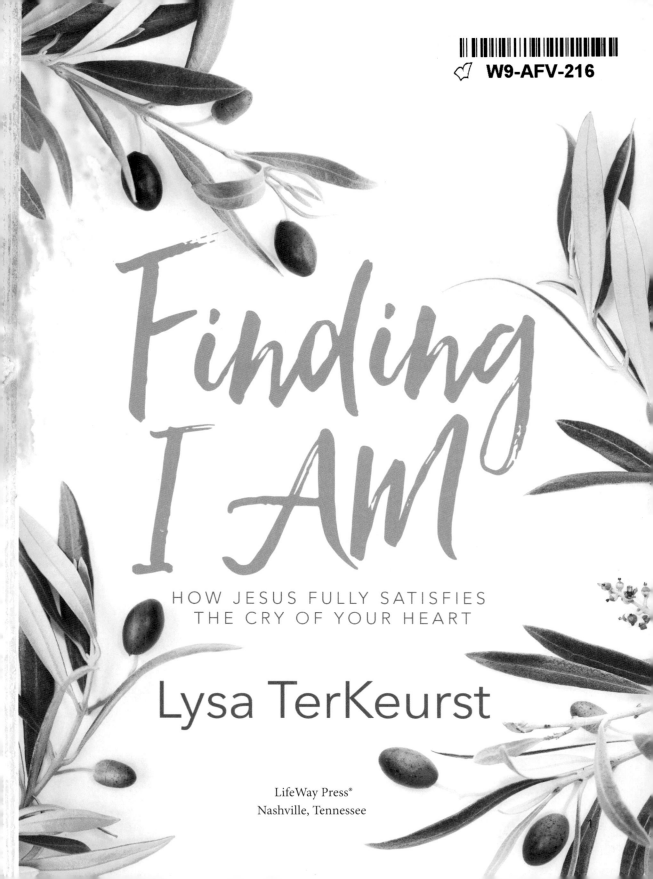

Finding I Am

HOW JESUS FULLY SATISFIES THE CRY OF YOUR HEART

Lysa TerKeurst

LifeWay Press®
Nashville, Tennessee

Published by LifeWay Press® • ©2016 Lysa TerKeurst
Reprinted October 2019

No part of this book may be reproduced or transmitted in any form or
by any means, electronic or mechanical, including photocopying and
recording, or by any information storage or retrieval system, except as may
be expressly permitted in writing by the publisher. Requests for permission
should be addressed in writing to LifeWay Press®; One LifeWay Plaza;
Nashville, TN 37234-0152.

ISBN 9781430053521
Item 005784578
Dewey decimal classification: 248.84
Subject heading: CHRISTIAN LIFE \ DISCIPLESHIP \ JESUS CHRIST—
TEACHINGS

Unless otherwise noted all Scripture quotations are from THE HOLY BIBLE,
NEW INTERNATIONAL VERSION®, NIV® Copyright © 1973, 1978, 1984, 2011
by Biblica, Inc.® Used by permission. All rights reserved worldwide. Scripture
quotations marked ESV are from The Holy Bible, English Standard Version®
(ESV®), copyright © 2001 by Crossway, a publishing ministry of Good News
Publishers. Used by permission.

To order additional copies of this resource, write LifeWay Church Resources
Customer Service; One LifeWay Plaza; Nashville, TN 37234-0113; FAX order
to 615.251.5933; call toll-free 800.458.2772; email *orderentry@lifeway.
com; or* order online at *www.lifeway.com.*

Printed in the United States of America

Adult Ministry Publishing, LifeWay Church Resources,
One LifeWay Plaza, Nashville, TN 37234-0152

CONTENTS

*HANDWRITING ON the WALL $5.00

MEET THE AUTHOR

Lysa TerKeurst is passionate about God's Word. She has studied extensively in the Holy Land and loves to make connections between the Old and New Testaments. Her deepest desire is to help others experience Jesus by unpacking Scripture in new and fresh ways everyone can understand!

Lysa is the president of Proverbs 31 Ministries and the #1 *New York Times* best-selling author of *Uninvited*, *The Best Yes*, and 20 other books. But to those who know her best she's just a simple girl who speaks about hope in the midst of her own struggles. Lysa lives with her family in Charlotte, North Carolina.

Connect with her at *www.LysaTerKeurst.com* or on social media @LysaTerKeurst.

INTRODUCTION

What is that relationship, that insecurity, that hurt, that desire, that prayer you've brought to God countless times? It's what makes you trust God the most, and in the not-so-spiritually-certain moments, it's what makes you most suspicious of Him. If God is good, why isn't He being good to you in answering this cry of your heart?

I've been there.

There is a desperate cry within my heart that I've longed with every fiber of my being to see come to pass. Minutes have turned into days and weeks and years of learning to make some sort of spiritual peace. On my good days I stand assured, "It's just not God's timing yet."

But on my less stellar days I crumble, afraid and hurt, "God, why? You know how much this ache in my heart steals a piece of too many of my smiles. Quite honestly, I'm tired of wondering if you're withholding because I'm not good enough, capable enough, spiritual enough, trusting enough, or mature enough. I guess I'm really tired of hoping."

This study is deeply personal to me. It's not a kumbaya, let's get together and just talk about the Bible enough to feel good about ourselves. This study is a lifeline, a way to get oxygen into the places of our hearts that have been starving to breathe and fully live.

And I'm so glad you are here to study with me. To search God's Word and seek Him as the source of our satisfaction.

In this study we are going to dive into the seven I AM statements of Jesus in the Gospel of John. We are going to go to places in the Holy Land where Jesus may have been when He uttered the words. I want the Word of God to come alive to you in this study—to reach the recesses of your heart because I truly believe that God's Word to us is life.

So, lean in with me, and let's see what Jesus wants to say to us and how He wants to satisfy our hearts.

ABOUT THIS STUDY

I fell in love with the Holy Land on my first trip to Israel a few years ago. In just two years, I've been there seven times studying and preparing to bring what I've learned to you. The Bible has come alive to me in a new way and one of my hopes in this study is that this will happen for you as well. This study was actually birthed out of one of my trips to Israel when the small group I was with specifically studied the Gospel of John. We heard our guide teach some of these I AM statements, and I left that trip knowing that I had to dive into this topic more fully.

In the study we will spend time on each of the I AM statements of Jesus in the Gospel of John. A few things you will want to know:

- The first video session is an introduction to the series.

- Then each week in your personal study time you will study one, or sometimes two, I AM statements.

- And then in the video following your week of study, I'll unpack the I AM statement(s) you just studied that week.

This was an intentional format because I want you to study the I AM statement for yourself, dig into Scripture on your own about each one, before I give you my thoughts on the subject.

You will have four days of personal study each week with an optional fifth day. That optional fifth day is just that, optional—don't feel like you have to do it. It's only if you want to take the study to the next level.

During the study we will be looking at many passages in the Gospel of John, but we won't be studying the whole book. What the optional fifth day of personal study will do is walk you through the entire Gospel of John a few chapters at a time. You may have already read some of the passages in that week of study, but in doing it this way you will read every word in the Gospel and be able to see the I AM statements in a fresh way because of it.

My prayer for you in this study is that you will discover that Jesus is the key to any kind of satisfaction you are looking for. He alone will fill the empty places in your heart, and I hope you find Him anew in this study. I'm so grateful to be taking this journey with you.

Jesus is the key to any kind of satisfaction you are looking for.

I AM THE *Bread* OF LIFE.

I AM THE *Light* OF THE WORLD.

I AM THE *Gate*.

I AM THE *Good Shepherd*.

I AM THE *Resurrection* AND THE *Life*.

I AM THE *Way* AND
THE *Truth* AND THE *Life*.

I AM THE TRUE *Vine*.

Video Session 1

WATCH VIDEO SESSION 1 AND RECORD YOUR NOTES BELOW.

Scripture in this video session: Exodus 3:1-15

Life WAY

Session I AM
Exodus 3:1-3 3:4-15

I AM - NAME
PROMISE   Romans ~~3008~~ 15:13

John

Video sessions available for purchase
at www.lifeway.com/findingIAM

group guide

VIDEO GROUP DISCUSSION QUESTIONS

After watching the video, discuss the following questions in your group.

1. God desires to be all <u>you</u> *need* and all you *want*. Describe the difference between the two from your own perspective.

2. Can you relate to the "sweet sorrow" I discussed in the video? Share any part of your story that you feel comfortable sharing that may be helpful to others.

   Jesus will come to you

3. How does the statement that <u>life isn't meant to fully satisfy us</u>, <u>only</u> Jesus can, speak to you today?

4. What are a few things you are hoping and praying for God to show you as you start this study?

   Patience –
   listening –
   caring
   obedience

   Gal 3:12
   col 5:22
   Roman 15:13
   John 6:35

Bread

I AM THE BREAD OF LIFE

JOHN 6:35

#FINDINGIAM

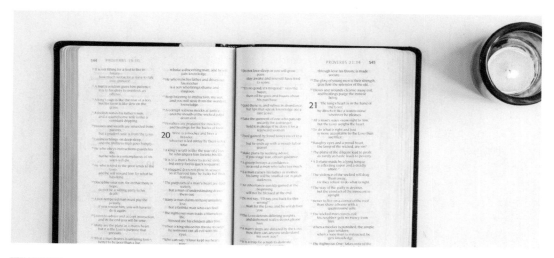

BIOS & ZOE LIFE

For years I've wanted to be like the spiritual giants who approach prayer and fasting with glee in their voices and a glide in their steps. They smile through the passing up of food with an apparent ease that's always eluded me. Yes, I wanted to be like them, but I was apparently too weak.

So, each time I heard about an invitation to fast from food I sidestepped the opportunity with my list of excuses:

I struggle with low blood sugar.

I get real grumpy when I get real hungry.

If I have an emotional breakdown while pursuing a spiritual breakthrough, it sort of defeats the purpose, you know?

I think fasting works for some people but not for me.

All I could think about was the struggle of my stomach. But then this past January something changed. I was feeling spiritually starved. Suddenly, all I could think about was the struggle of my heart.

There was a desperation like I'd never known as I confronted the source of my ache. I reached a place where I could not hear from God. I felt disconnected from believing God's promises were true for me personally. I was desperate to have relief from this unbelief.

I could sense His presence. I could connect with His truth. What I longed for the most, His voice of assurance and instruction, was stunningly silent.

That thing I mentioned in the introduction—the source of my holy wrestling, my silent suffering, the reason my pillow was sometimes wet with tears, the pain—was at an all time high. And then suddenly and almost cruelly, God seemed eerily silent.

I lay in bed one night racked with an imploding feeling.

One sleepless night turned into 2, 3, 7, 10. Starvation of the soul doesn't give permission slips for sleep to help you escape its grip.

I cried at unusual times. I withdrew from depth in my conversations with others. I lied about having a sore throat, a sour stomach, a bug of some sort—anything to excuse me from having to be present.

When you are absent in heart but present in reality, you know the slightest bump or jostle by anyone would shatter your ability to hold it together. You'd be nothing but dust that even a wisp of wind could and would blow away without any sympathy at all. As everything about you goes flying, you'd suddenly and horrifically realize you're helpless to gather the particles that were once "you" back into something of any sort of substance.

And then on night 11, finally, I slept. Physically, I felt better the next day. But spiritually I was so utterly exhausted and spent that I knew something had to break through. That's when another fasting invitation came.

Out of nothing but sheer desperation I said yes: "Yes, God, I will fast from food that gives me physical comfort so I can find something new with You. I don't want comfort. I want connection. I must hear from You. It's not even an option to go one more day without feeding my soul with Your whisper."

I didn't do a complete fast. But it was more than I'd ever been willing to try before. I was desperate. It's amazing the powerful influence desperation can have on a person for good or bad. Desperation can lead to degradation.

Desperate people can find themselves doing desperately degrading things to ease their source of pain. But desperation for God is different. True desperation for God will lead to revelation.

And after only a few days the revelation I got stunned me.

God was *allowing* this source of pain in my life.

Apart from Him there is no true satisfaction.

He wasn't causing it. He didn't take pleasure in it. He didn't like the hurt it was causing me. But He absolutely was allowing it. And the only whisper from God that kept rushing through my heart was that I had to learn to fully trust Him and Him alone.

Without full trust in Him, it is impossible to be fully satisfied by Him. And apart from Him, there is no fullness. Apart from Him there is no true satisfaction.

The instant fix I had been begging Him to give me would only benefit me in physical and emotional realms. It would have given me a temporary fix and a brief stint of relief, but it would never develop in me a permanent source of life from which to draw upon time and again.

God was after so much more for me. He was after my soul. That deeper place where God wants to ease the hunger of our souls can only be accessed when we are stripped of the cheaper, temporary sources of nourishment.

In John 6:35, we find God personalizing His original "I AM" statement from Exodus 3 through His Son's declaration.

TAKE A MOMENT AND READ JOHN 6:35.

> Then Jesus declared, "I am the bread of life. Whoever comes to me will never go hungry, and whoever believes in me will never be thirsty."
> JOHN 6:35

Remember, God's "I AM" statement from Exodus was so completely full that it needed no qualifier. It was the promise that His presence was everything we ever needed. It was all peace, all provision, all perfection, and all protection. That was His promise given. But our human hearts were designed by God not just for His completion but also for His companionship. We needed His promise and His presence to be personalized.

Jesus and His seven I AM statements from John personalize God's promises.

Make no mistake, God is I AM. He is absolutely all we need, but He delights in us not only needing Him but also wanting Him.

So, He gives us something we've craved physically on a daily basis since the beginning of time—bread. But He isn't just any bread. He's the Bread of life.

There are two words for *life* in the Bible. One is *bios*, used 10 times in the Bible, which means "breath in your lungs or physical life." The other is *zoe*, which means "possessed with vitality looking to the fullness of life." It's used 135 times in the Bible.[1]

> Let's look up one verse for each of these words to get an idea of how they are used. Look up the following verses and write some ways the word is used according to the passage.
>
> *Bios*: Luke 21:4
>
>
> *Zoe*: 1 John 5:12   *John 10:10*

Why do you think *zoe* is used 125 times more than *bios*?

· *Prefer to Life*

Jesus doesn't want us to just live with breath in our lungs walking around as a shell of existence. He wants us to have a rare vitality, experiencing the fullness of soul someone should experience when Jesus Himself does everyday life with us.

 Do you believe this? Do you believe Jesus wants this for you? Why or why not?

I believe it for me. I believe it for you. Because before the beginning of time, God has waited for you to read these words and come to this realization. That thing you've been so desperate to see come to pass? That unanswered prayer? That unrelenting ache? The cries you're so afraid are unheard? The unyielding addiction? That unsung recognition? Your unraveling hope?

Those answers and the easing of that ache aren't the source of finally becoming fully satisfied. They aren't. And you believing this lie is a scheme of Satan to keep you in an unsatisfied place.

Trust me, even if that problem was solved, the enemy has another waiting in the wings that will be just as distracting and devastating to you as this one. We live in a broken world where escaping brokenness isn't possible. Our souls were made for the perfection of the garden; therefore, they can't ever be satisfied by the imperfect grit and grind of this sin-soaked world.

I have a theory about why I've anguished and suffered so desperately through this message. Because Satan wants to steal these words, kill my desire to deliver them, and destroy the miracles this teaching will produce in my life and in yours. The enemy of our soul strategizes day and night to get us to settle for *bios* life so we will never taste the hell-shattering fullness of *zoe*.

It's been his plan since the beginning.

We see it when the Bread of life was tempted by the enemy in the desert.

TAKE A MOMENT AND READ MATTHEW 4:1-4.

Jesus had been fasting for forty days and the Scriptures make sure to note that "he was hungry" (v. 2). So, the enemy tempts Jesus to satisfy His *bios* need—eat some physical bread—so that He would starve His *zoe* need—the deep satisfaction of fasting for deeper connection with God.

In what way has the enemy been tempting you to satisfy physical and emotional needs and kept you from pursuing that *zoe* life we've been reading about?

We need both *bios* life and *zoe* life. It's not one or the other—it's a "both and" deal. But we must remember it can't just be *bios* life. We were also made for *zoe*. As a matter of fact, I think God uses our hunger for *bios* bread to give us a picture of *zoe* bread. Think about the way physical hunger works. Hunger isn't a bad thing. Hunger produces a need for provision.

Physical hunger produces a need for what kind of provision?

Doesn't it make sense that God would also allow us to experience spiritual hunger as well? What does the term *spiritual hunger* mean to you?

Just like we read in Matthew 4 where the tempter came to twist the truth with Jesus, he will want to twist the truth of God's provision for us. God is the source of life through His provision. The enemy is the source of lies through his perversion.

What we consume will consume us. It's our choice whether we are consuming God's life or the enemy's lies.

God is the source of life through His provision.

Write out <u>Matthew 6:33 here</u>:

The word *seek* in the original Greek is the word *zeteo* which means "to crave."[2]

What are you truly craving today?

A declaration is "a positive, explicit, or formal statement."[3] Write out your personal declaration of what you need to shift or give up in order to crave the Bread of life like never before.

FEEDING THE 5,000

4th miracle

Before Jesus utters His first official I AM statement, He performs a miracle—the feeding of the 5,000. This is the fourth miracle of Jesus in the Book of John, but the first I AM statement. Before we can truly understand the I AM statement, we need to look at the miracle.

John 6 is where we will camp out this week. Even if you are unfamiliar with Jesus and the Gospels, you have probably heard of the feeding of the 5,000. After all, it is the only miracle that we read about in all four Gospels. For that reason alone we should sit up and take note.

PLEASE READ JOHN 6:1-9.

Why were the crowds following Jesus? (v. 2)

Imagine hearing about a man like that in your life today. What would be the request you would make of Him?

Look specifically at verse 4. In what time of year did this occur?

Passover was a springtime festival that celebrated the deliverance of the Hebrew people (Israelites) from Egypt where they were held in bondage as slaves. Take a moment and consider the feeding of the 5,000 within the context of this festival. Passover celebrates God as a deliverer. During the Israelites' wandering in the desert God provided manna from heaven. Don't miss this important point. This was one of the biggest times of celebration on the Jewish calendar. In fact, it was the highlight of their spiritual history. And not only did they celebrate and look back to thank God for what He had done, they also, perhaps just as importantly, looked forward to when God would send another prophet like Moses to bring deliverance to them.

Little did they know that the very Prophet they were waiting for was in their midst. Do you think they wondered if it was Him? Do you think they had hope stirring within them that maybe this would be the One who would rescue them and deliver them once and for all? Or do you think the many years of waiting with no result had hardened their hearts so much that they didn't really believe anymore? Were they just celebrating to celebrate or did it have purpose?

> What promise from God are you waiting to be fulfilled? Or what have you asked God for time after time with no tangible results?
>
> *Pain Relief*

Maybe you'd like to start this study with a simple prayer for God to open your heart and soften it. I'd like to challenge you with something I challenged myself with as I worked through this material. Pray every day of this study for God to open and soften your heart to hear from Him. Ask Him to help you to trust Him. Keep hoping, keep praying, and keep watching for His hand. Just because you don't clearly see God's work at this moment does not mean He is not working.

WITH THAT IN MIND, LET'S LOOK BACK AT JOHN 6:5-9.

Poor Philip. He is trying so hard. And then Andrew gave his own shot at a plan. Neither were even close to a good solution. They were hopeless. Feeding these people was, to them, an impossible situation.

> Why do you think Jesus asked Philip where they should buy the bread for the people if He already knew the answer?

How have you seen God show up in a seemingly impossible situation in your life or in the life of someone you know?

READ THE REST OF THE STORY IN JOHN 6:10-15.

Look closely at verse 11. All Jesus does here is give thanks. He simply says the blessing. The blessing that He might have said, according to Jewish tradition could have been:

 "Blessed be thou, Yahweh our God, king of the world who causes bread to come forth from earth."[4]

Hillside near Capernaum

Maybe this doesn't speak to you like it does to me, but I love how a blessing opens up this miracle. Thanking God for what He has done. For who He is. Thankfulness opened the door to what God had in store for this group of 5,000.

Maybe you feel too heartbroken to be thankful.
Maybe you feel too hurt to be thankful.
Maybe you feel too fearful to be thankful.
Maybe you feel too disappointed to be thankful.
Maybe you feel too mad to be thankful.
Maybe you feel too depressed to be thankful.
Maybe you feel too hopeless to be thankful.

Fill in the blank for yourself:
I feel too _____ to be thankful.

The solution to your problem or issue may be thankfulness. It's at least worth a try, don't you think?

Jesus provided food to the people on this hillside after He thanked God. They ate and enjoyed what was likely much-needed nourishment. They had full stomachs and now their ears were open and ready to hear from Jesus. And I'm certainly glad they were ready to listen because Jesus was going to challenge their thinking with what He was about to say.

Before we close out this day of study, though, I want us to look at a few things about the feeding of the 5,000 from the perspective of Mark's Gospel. Let me start by telling you a story.

I'm not sure when it happened. I can't pinpoint a moment or a skewed thought or a wrong perspective that started it. But I'm now well aware that somewhere along the journey of my long wrestling through my unanswered prayer, my heart started to harden.

> The hushing of humility will be the rushing in of pride.

Like I said, I can't tell you when it happened, but I can tell you the first clue to realizing it's happening to you: It's when you hush humility.

The hushing of humility will be the rushing in of pride. There's nothing that crystallizes and encrusts the soft places of a heart more than the subtle first notions that you disagree with truth.

You start to think you deserve a little more than truth will allow.

You begin to believe you know a little better than the truth that bumps up against your desire.

You excuse away the promptings that your justifications to skew truth aren't so justified.

From that platform an elevated sense of self grows.

The disciples found themselves in just this predicament.

They'd been out doing public ministry with great success. And then they stumble upon the feeding of the 5,000. They had served Jesus in the big ways of preaching, teaching, healing, and casting out demons, but would they still serve Jesus in the quiet places that weren't so glamorous? In other words, was their service still about serving God, or was it about serving their egos?

LET'S READ MARK'S VERSION OF THE STORY.
READ MARK 6:30-42.

Write down what the disciples are telling Jesus.

What was Jesus' immediate reaction to what they were telling Him? Did He praise their efforts? Did He encourage them to do more? Or did He look into their souls and see a different kind of need?

In verse 36 we find that the disciples relied on their own human logic to solve the problem. What did they suggest?

What does this tell us about their understanding of who Jesus is?

NOW TAKE A LOOK AT MARK 6:49-52.

What was the most tragic thing a hardened heart caused them to miss?

How does this speak to you personally?

Don't miss the timing that right after this event as John tells it is when Jesus reveals Himself as the Bread of life—the source of zoe fullness in John 6:35. Astoundingly intentional if you ask me!

DAY 3

BREAD

You might be a little disappointed in what I'm about to tell you. I realize I left you with a cliffhanger yesterday. We are going to wait and cover the answer to the cliffhanger, though, on Day 4. I know, I know. But trust me, it will be worth the wait. We have to study the word *bread* first because it is fascinating and it helps us appreciate what Jesus says in John 6.

Can you bear with me one more day, then? I really hope so.

Remember, Jesus didn't just pull these I AM statements out of the air for no particular reason nor because they just happened to pop in His head. No, they were quite deliberate. And they all point back to the Old Testament. Today we are going to spend some time looking back at other places in Scripture that speak of bread and see what God might teach us.

BREAD AS A CONSEQUENCE

You can't get three chapters into Genesis before we see the first mention of the word *bread*. At this point God has created the world, and Adam and Eve, and has given them the only rule they had to obey—don't eat from the tree of the knowledge of good and evil. I'm guessing you remember what happens. The serpent enters. Satan stirs doubt ("Did God really say?" Gen. 3:1). They listen to him. And they break the rule.

I love what the theologian Sinclair Ferguson says about this instance in our spiritual history: "The lie was an assault on both God's generosity and his integrity. Neither his character nor his words were to be trusted. This, in fact, is the lie that sinners have believed ever since—the lie of the not-to-be-trusted-because-he-does-not-love-me-false-Father."[5] When you really get to the bottom of why Adam and Eve listened to the serpent you find they (like us at times) didn't believe what God said to be true and didn't believe God had the best in mind for them.

Sin entered. And the consequences of this cataclysmic choice came to light. Let's pick up there.

READ GENESIS 3:8-24. LOOK FOR THE WORD BREAD (SOME TRANSLATIONS MAY SAY FOOD).

Note how bread (or food) was a part of sin's consequence.

Reading this account made me think: *How did they get food before this?* We don't know for sure, but probably they gathered food from trees. In Genesis 2:15, we see that God placed man in the garden to work it and watch over it, but somehow after the fall, the ground was cursed. With sin entering, they now must work for their bread in a different way—"by the sweat of your brow" (v. 19). Not easy work. Hard work. Work that has no end.

BREAD AS A PROVISION

When bread was introduced as a result of Adam and Eve's sin in Genesis 3, they soon realized it was something they would have to work for. Grain would first have to be gathered, sifted, cleaned, and ground to make flour. It was only after these laborious steps that the flour would be mixed with water and kneaded to form cakes that could then be baked to make bread. While the process involved multiple steps, it was still a process that God ordained to provide the people with food.

The story of the Israelites gives us a better glimpse into God's gracious provision of bread. Bread was a staple in the Israelites' diet. They came to depend on it.

After 400 years of slavery, 10 plagues, and a journey across the Red Sea, the Israelites found themselves free from the Egyptians. But their travels also left them unable to collect new grain, and the grain they had brought with them from Egypt soon ran out. In Exodus 16, we see their reaction to this predicament.

When they found themselves without the grain to make bread, they panicked. They panicked because they did not remember the promise. They did not remember how God had provided for them all along. So instead of crying out to God to provide and sustain, they grumbled and accused Moses and Aaron of bringing them out from under Egyptian slavery only to leave them to die of starvation in the wilderness.

Yet amidst the grumbling and panicked pleas of the Israelites, God heard and graciously provided. A special bread known as *manna* would rain down from heaven each day.

Why do you think God chose to provide for the Israelites in this specific way?

I love that the Lord provided for His people in this way. Think about it. There is no rationale or even natural explanation for something like manna. I can't help but think that if bread appeared from the ground the Israelites would have been tempted to rationalize and even devalue the provision of God. I think they may have had the tendency to explain it away rather than see the mercy and provision of God. You see, God could have fed them any way He saw fit, but by choosing to rain the manna down from heaven, He was reminding the people that He alone was their Provider. He was shifting their focus from the ground (their own efforts to provide) to the heavens (God's ability to provide). He was lifting their eyes to Him.

Do you have a similar story? Has there been a time in your life where God clearly provided for you in a way that only He could? Explain.

Whether you have a big story with which to remember God's providing for you or it's a more simple example, He is faithful. Just the fact that we are sitting here today breathing and able to be together is rich evidence of God's faithfulness. This helps me lift my eyes when my heart aches over my not-yet-answered prayer. Looking at His faithfulness to provide helps me see if He did it before, He will do it again. Or maybe His delayed answer is actually His best provision for me right now.

How does that resonate with you?

Let's look at a time when the Israelites celebrated God providing in the past, which gave them hope that He could provide again.

THE FESTIVAL OF UNLEAVENED BREAD

The Book of Leviticus outlines many of the Israelite laws and holy days—the laws and celebrations that would *set them apart* from the rest of the world at that time. These laws and celebrations also *set them up* to remember God's actions in their lives.

READ THE VERSES BELOW AND FILL IN THE NAME OF THE FESTIVAL IN THE COLUMN ON THE LEFT.[6]

NAME	DATE	REFERENCE	SIGNIFICANCE
	Mar/Apr: 14-21	Ex. 12:2-20; Lev. 23:5	Commemorates God's deliverance of Israel out of Egypt.
	Mar/Apr: 15-21	Lev. 23:6-8	Commemorates God's deliverance of Israel out of Egypt. Includes a Day of Firstfruits for the barley harvest.
	May/June: 6 (seven weeks after Passover)	Ex. 23:16; 34:22; Lev. 23:15-21	Commemorates the giving of the law at Mount Sinai. Includes a Day of Firstfruits for the wheat harvest.
	Sept/Oct: 1	Lev. 23:23-25; Num. 29:1-6	Day of the blowing of the trumpets to signal the beginning of the civil new year.
	Sept/Oct: 10	Ex. 30:10; Lev. 23:26-33	On this day the high priest makes atonement for the nation's sin. Also a day of fasting.
	Sept/Oct: 15-21	Lev. 23:33-43; Num. 29:12-39; Deut. 16:13	Commemorates the forty years of wilderness wandering.
	Nov/Dec: 25-30; and Tebeth, Dec/Jan: 1-2	John 10:22	Commemorates the purification of the temple by Judas Maccabeaus in 164 B.C.
	Feb/Mar: 14	Esther 9:26	Commemorates the deliverance of the Jewish people in the days of Esther.

Unleavened bread

If you want to read more about the rest of the holy celebrations you can do that by just finishing out Leviticus 23.

The Festival of Unleavened Bread (which is celebrated during the month of Passover) was on the fifteenth day of the first month and was a reminder to the Israelites how God delivered them from slavery in Egypt. You might remember that they made unleavened bread and left with haste once God delivered them (Ex. 12:17-20). The Festival of Unleavened Bread offered a yearly opportunity to remember and celebrate the deliverance of God's people. It was also a time to sacrifice firstfruits to the Lord, including a grain offering. This gift was a sacrifice and a reminder that everything the Israelites had was from the Lord.

When Jesus entered the scene, Passover and the Festival of Unleavened Bread were no longer two distinct festivals but rather were celebrated together. By that time, it was the greatest Jewish national holiday the Israelites celebrated.[7]

In the Old Testament every firstborn, human or animal, belonged to God (Ex. 13:2), so the "firstfruits," or initial yield of every crop, were set aside as an offering. And the offering was also an indicator of the harvest that one would reap. Likewise, Jesus was the offering on our behalf. Because He rose from the grave during this well-known Jewish festival, we have a clear, beautiful picture of Jesus being the grain/bread offering in our stead.

THE HOUSE OF BREAD

We've only just scratched the surface of the fascinating references to the word *bread* in the Bible, but this will be our last exercise on the subject today. Jesus was born in Bethlehem. The word *Bethlehem* means "house of bread." Don't lose the significance here: The house of bread was where the Bread of life was born. God knew Jesus would be the Bread of life, and He chose for Him to be born in the city bearing that same name.

Bread as a consequence to sin in Genesis becomes our salvation in a city so many thousands of years later. Jesus was certainly deliberate as He named these I AM statements in the Book of John. Each one is important, significant, and rich for our lives today. In our time tomorrow we will study the first time Jesus opens His mouth and declares, "I AM."

THE BREAD OF LIFE WALKS ON WATER

Unrealistic expectations often lead to our greatest frustrations. I wonder sometimes if part of my wrestling through the desperate cry of my heart is that I want life to satisfy me. I have an unrealistic expectation that life should tie up in a tidy bow, like the nursery rhyme that says,

Row, row, row your boat

Gently down the stream

Merrily, merrily, merrily, merrily

Life is but a dream.

This nursery rhyme and children's song was first printed in 1852. I'm sure you know it well, either from memories in your childhood, or maybe you sing it with children in your life now. Like many nursery rhymes, though, I never really stop to think about the lyrics. It has become so ingrained in our culture that I just sing it without thinking.

Have you ever rowed a boat? I don't think *gently* is a word that I would use to describe it. Instead I think of words like: *tiresome, hard work, difficult.* And then that last lyric—"life is but a dream." It sounds nice, but it's just not true.

Life is not always smooth. The stream is not always easy to row. You know this. Jesus did, too. And while we are out on the waters of life, Jesus shows up—not in a boat, but walking.

Remember that before Jesus said any of His I AM statements He first performed five miracles. We discussed the fourth miracle on Day 2. Today we get to talk about the fifth miracle and then finally look at Jesus' first I AM statement. If you'll recall we saw earlier this week that John 6:1-15 ends with Jesus escaping from the crowd that wanted to make Him king. He went away to be alone.

LET'S PICK UP AT THAT POINT AND READ JOHN 6:16-21.

Many of the disciples were fishermen, so they would have had lots of experience navigating from one side of the sea to another. But before they could reach the other side, a massive storm rolled in. Rough winds caused the sea to rise and the boat to be rocked. Despite the disciples' initial willingness, worry began to set in. I imagine many began to wonder why Jesus would leave them alone during such a scary time. But before their fears could grow any further, Jesus came to their aid by walking on the water and getting into the boat. He became the answer to their need. Maybe I would be less frustrated if I understood that Jesus is my satisfaction—not a more tidy life.

As Jesus stepped into the boat, another miraculous thing happened.

What was it (see v. 21)?

When we're going through a storm, we often try to face it ourselves. We pull out the tools we have in our tool belt and start fighting the battle. Frustration, exhaustion, and exasperation set in. Finally, we ask Jesus to help us. He has everything we need to win this battle and overcome this struggle. We can trust Him. So I wonder why we so often make Him a last resort rather than our first response?

What storms have you tried to face on your own? What battles have you tried to fight without turning to Jesus?

What are your go-to "tools" that you pull out when you get into this kind of situation?

Speaking of this passage of Scripture, author Michael Card said, "Chapter 6 is the hinge on which the story of John's Gospel turns. It marks a radical shift in Jesus' ministry: from His greatest moment of acceptance and popularity to one of the darkest instances of offense and rejection."[8]

This section of Scripture marks a huge turning point in Jesus' ministry. After walking with the people and performing miracles, He is finally about to start telling people about Himself. And their response was much like many today. Either they embraced Him or they rejected Him.

PLEASE READ JOHN 6:22-42.

Why did Jesus say the crowds were following Him (see v. 26)?

Do you think people would try to fill their spiritual hunger if all their physical needs were continually met? Why or why not?

There is a difference in coming to Jesus for bread and because He is Bread.

Since you are walking with me through this study, I have a feeling that you are following after Jesus. But this passage makes me stop and question, *Why am I following Jesus? Is it so that I can get something from Him? Am I like the crowds who simply want their bellies filled? Or am I coming to Him because He is Bread to me?* There is a difference in coming to Jesus for bread and because He is Bread.

The crowd asks Jesus what they can do to perform the works of God. What a bold question! And Jesus answered right back with a bold response— "The work of God is this: to believe in the one he has sent" (John 6:29). Believing is the work. And that can be hard sometimes because we can't measure belief. We can't check belief off a to-do list. Belief can't be seen and praised by those around us. Belief is in our hearts. Only God truly sees what we believe.

> How can you guard against the seemingly never ending to-do list of what you think you should do as a "good Christian"? How can you remind yourself that believing in Jesus is all you need?

The crowd then brings up the manna in the wilderness. Begging Jesus to give them a sign so they can believe. They even gave Him a helpful hint—why not do what Moses did and provide manna from heaven?

Oh, the manna. The bread from heaven that came down every morning to feed the Israelites when they were in the wilderness. Day after day it came. God was teaching the Israelites that He was the ultimate Provider. As they wandered through the wilderness, they had to rely on God every day in order to live, for He only provided enough manna for each day.

But the manna of the Old Testament was just a shadow of the Bread that was to come.

In the Gospel of John we see that Jesus did more than the manna ever could. Jesus was the true living Bread that came down from heaven. He said, "Whoever comes to me will never go hungry" (John 6:35).

We see the difference between Jesus and manna in the miracle of the feeding of the 5,000. Twelve baskets were left over. Jesus is not only the Provider, He is the Bread of life who never runs out and gives you exceedingly, abundantly more than you can imagine. All you have to do is believe.

OPTIONAL

For those of you who are able to take this study a little deeper, I invite you to read the Gospel of John. I think you will really enjoy reading through the entire Gospel account to get a fuller picture of the I AM statements. (Please note: We won't be discussing your Day 5 reflections in the group study as it is an optional activity.)

For today's portion please read John 1–4. Then, use this page to record any thoughts, prayers, or things you want to remember from the reading.

Good questions to ask as you read are:
What does this passage teach me about God?

_____

_____

_____

_____

_____

_____

_____

_____

What does this passage teach me about myself?

_____

_____

_____

_____

_____

_____

_____

_____

What do I need to do as a result of reading this passage?

_____

_____

_____

_____

_____

_____

_____

As you read John today, see which of these attributes of God are exemplified and write out any thoughts you have about them.

Compassionate	Good	Faithful	Holy	Patient	Wise
Generous	Loving	Just	True	All-Knowing	
All-Powerful	Eternal	Gracious	Merciful	Faithful	

_____

_____

_____

_____

_____

_____

_____

_____

_____

_____

_____

_____

_____

Video Session 2

WATCH VIDEO SESSION 2 AND RECORD YOUR NOTES BELOW.

Scripture in this video session:
Matt. 4:13-16 • Jer. 25:10-11 • Rev. 18:22 • John 6:1-35 • Matt. 6

_____
_____
_____
_____
_____
_____
_____
_____
_____
_____
_____
_____
_____
_____
_____
_____
_____
_____
_____
_____

VIDEO GROUP DISCUSSION QUESTIONS

After watching the video, discuss the following questions in your group.

1. Start by reading Matthew 6 in its entirety and ask, *How can what I'm reading now be daily bread to me? How can I make these words, His words, become part of who I am today? How can I make these words redirect the way I live today?*

2. When you no longer hear the grinding of wheat for daily bread, it's a sound of desolation. How does this knowledge fall on you today?

3. We all too often fill ourselves on other breads. The bread of works. The bread of performance. The bread of achievement or attention. Jesus gives us more than those breads ever will. Jesus gives us the bread of life. What "bread" are you going to and how can you be reminded that Jesus gives us the true bread of life?

4. Describe the difference between ingesting the words of God and digesting them. How can you digest God's words more this week?

5. How do you respond to the statement: "The more we enjoy Jesus, the more we will crave Him"? How does that speak to you?

Light

I AM THE LIGHT OF THE WORLD

JOHN 8:12

#FINDINGIAM

THE FESTIVAL OF TABERNACLES
AND THE LIVING WATER

Do you ever wonder exactly what God wants you to do, especially when you have so many options and demands to manage?

So often, we want big directional signs from God. But God just wants us to pay attention to what He places right in front of us. I learned this early on in ministry when I had dreams to do big things for God.

However, when I looked at what was right in front of me at that time, I saw my neighbors, Ken and Mary. They lived right down the street and were known for their amazing hospitality, adorable farmhouse, and parties that stepped out of the pages of a magazine. Mary was alive with creativity and always thinking of ways to bless others. Ken adored living out his retirement years helping his bride create a haven for family and friends.

But cancer swept in and before long, Ken laid Mary to rest in the arms of Jesus.

I remember seeing Ken not long after Mary's funeral. I knew I needed to stop and say something. But what? When I reached Ken, I just gave him a hug. "How are you, Ken?" Tears filled his eyes, "Not so good. The silence is killing me, Lysa."

And with those words, I knew this interaction with Ken was an assignment from God. He was stirring my heart more and more as I began to sense I was to invite Ken over for dinner.

I started having this argument with God in my mind, *God, he's going to expect food. Cooking isn't in my Top 10 talents. I mean, sometimes we just order pizza and call it a night. My cooking doesn't even come close to Mary's. Are you sure about this?*

But Ken hadn't asked for an amazing meal. What made his heart ache was the silence.

So I smiled at Ken and said, "Well then, you must come to our house for dinner. I can't always promise it will be tidy and I'm certainly no great cook, but one thing is for sure—my house is never silent."

Thus started a tradition—Monday night dinners with Ken.

We never had candles or tablecloths or even a properly set table. But the noise of our family was an orchestra of comfort and healing to Ken's lonely heart.

Being knee-deep in the realities of small children made me feel like this wasn't my season of life to make a difference to the outside world. But God used my offering of what little I had!

We just did life and let Ken join in. I would often ask about Mary's ways of doing things, and his face would light up at the opportunity to keep part of her alive. And slowly but surely, as we all made time for these special dinners, we recaptured the sacredness of relationships that so often gets lost in the rush of our days.

One night, as Ken was leaving our home, he stepped off the sidewalk to make his way over to a bush in full bloom. He tenderly picked up one of the flowers and pressed his face close, breathing in its scent deeply. He then looked back at me standing in the doorway and said, "Don't miss this. Don't rush through your life, Lysa. Make time to stop and breathe it all in." I've never forgotten that.

Eventually, Ken met someone who could cook, got remarried, and moved away. But my family and I still preserve that sacred space for Monday night dinner tradition. We invite coworkers, acquaintances, and friends who feel like family to join us. We take time to talk. Laugh. Process life. Breathe it all in. Although our to-do lists and schedules tug at our attention, we don't allow anything to take priority over these moments. I refuse to let the people I've been entrusted with get my "less" instead of my "best" because I'm distracted.

A little gift placed in the hands of a big God can change the world.

I'm so thankful God entrusted me with that small assignment to give Ken noise all those years ago. A little gift placed in the hands of a big God can change the world. It changed ours, and it changed Ken's. It's amazing to me that what started out as a simple gesture to help a grieving neighbor became one of the greatest ministry blessings to me and my family. And I've done a lot of "breathing it all in" like Ken instructed ever since.

What kind of traditions do you hold dear in your family now or from your family growing up?

During the time of Jesus, the Feast of the Tabernacles was an important occasion in the life of the Jewish people. If you were the type of family that attended this festival, then you most likely had traditions to go along with it. Little did the Jewish people know, though, that this particular year the Feast of Tabernacles would be quite different—because at this one, Jesus was going to reveal who He is.

John 7 takes place during the Feast of the Tabernacles and you can feel the controversy, confusion, and speculation that came with Jesus attending the festival. He made some bold claims that concerned the Jewish leaders of the day.

Everyone seemed to have an opinion about Jesus. Some people flat out didn't like Him. Some people wanted to believe Him but really struggled to understand His words. Some people stuck by Him. I wonder how Jesus got through this time in His ministry. Saying things that were true but so hard for people to understand. He was astounding them with His words. And the people did not know how to take it.

TAKE A FEW MINUTES TO READ JOHN 7:1-36. TRY TO PICTURE IT IN YOUR HEAD AS IF YOU WERE THERE, SO YOU CAN SENSE THE TENSION FOR YOURSELF.

Record a few words and phrases that stood out to you about the scene.

(You may have noticed in verse 8 that Jesus says He isn't going to the festival. Then in verse 10 He sets out for the festival. If we read verse 8 in its original Greek, we get a better explanation of what seems to be a contradiction. The Greek gives the sense that Jesus said "I am not now going" which would explain why He did not go with his brothers but instead went alone at a later time.)

The Feast of Tabernacles, during which the action in John 7 takes place, is sometimes called the Feast of Booths. Two aspects of this feast were front and center for the Jewish people: water and light.

Booths were constructed of fresh branches of trees. The Feast of Tabernacles is still celebrated today.

The Feast of the Tabernacles was the most joyous and the longest festival in the Jewish calendar—it lasted eight days in the early fall (September/October).[1] It was a time to celebrate the last of the year's harvest and was also a time to commemorate God faithfully providing for His people during the time the Israelites spent in the wilderness.

The festival was characterized by three major events:

1. Participating in a procession of palms;
2. Observing as the priests daily poured water from the fountain of Siloam onto the altar;
3. Illuminating four large menorahs each night in the temple courts.

After a sacrifice, the very next thing that would happen in the morning was pouring the libation of water upon the altar. And the last thing that would happen at night was the torch dance; it lasted up until dawn. Water and Light.

Now remember the controversy we just read about in John 7. People wanted to seize Jesus. Common sense might tell you this was the time to back down and take a back seat for a while—let the crowd simmer down. But that is not the direction Jesus chose.

TAKE A LOOK FOR YOURSELF AND READ JOHN 7:37-44.

There is no official "I AM" statement here, but list what Jesus does say about Himself.

List some of the reactions to this statement by the crowd.

This is the first time Jesus said this kind of statement in front of a crowd. But it is not the first time He said it. He said it first in His encounter with the Samaritan woman recorded in John 4.

Keep in mind the two major elements of the Feast of the Tabernacles—water and light. The priests knew the symbolism of the water because they knew the Old Testament Scriptures well. Isaiah 55:1 says: "Come, all you who are thirsty, come to the waters; and you who have no money, come, buy and eat! Come, buy wine and milk without money and without cost."

Every morning during the festival the priests would proceed from the Temple Mount down to the spring of Siloam. They would travel down with a large golden pitcher and draw water with it. When the priest got back to the Temple Mount the crowd and the priests would greet him saying, "With joy shall ye draw water out of the wells of salvation."[2]

Every year during this festival they would do this. They would say these words. But, this particular time, it's one of the saddest things I've ever heard because the well of salvation was in their midst and they didn't even recognize it.

Never again will we be thirsty if we come to Jesus to drink. Bread last week. Water today. The living water Jesus spoke of is the gift of salvation, fullness of life. A free gift to us but a gift that cost Jesus His life.

It grieves me that there are so many people in this world going to a well day after day to fill up their bucket with water that won't last. You always get thirsty again. You always need water. You need it every. single. day.

What wells do you think our culture tries to draw water from on a regular basis?

What wells are you tempted to draw satisfaction from on a regular basis?

Do we look to work, family, education, various achievements? If we are honest with ourselves, we find a flickering and fleeting sense of satisfaction from these, but none of them can be the full source of satisfaction in our lives. They can quench part of our heart but never reach that deep thirst of the soul. Only Jesus can do that. Jesus is the source of satisfaction that will not leave us wanting.

There is nothing you have to do to obtain the fullness of life; you just have to receive it. The Holy Spirit who comes upon us at our salvation is miraculous. This doesn't mean we will always feel content and never feel dissatisfaction. The promise that Jesus gives us is enough. The way I've seen Him work in my life and bring living water to my soul in the driest of seasons is enough for me to keep putting one foot in front of the other and trusting Him. And step by step, my soul is beginning to feel hopeful again. Like I might be able to make real progress in this journey.

So I hold onto the faithfulness of my God. And unlike the priests of this time drawing water from a well that will never satisfy, I look to Jesus and say, "With joy shall ye draw water out of the wells of salvation." Amen and amen.

Spend a few moments today as we close out our time together confessing to God your tendency to draw water from wells other than Jesus. Write about the progress you sense that you're making and some ways that you need to draw living water today.

I AM THE LIGHT OF THE WORLD

Yesterday we talked about a special Jewish celebration and some distinct parts of that feast. Let's do a quick recap.

What festival were the Jews celebrating?

What happened in the morning during this feast?

Let's fast forward now to the end of the day during this time of celebration.

The torch dance ends the day during the Feast of Tabernacles. Here is the scene. The dance takes place in the court of women in the temple. See the diagram of the temple on page 50 and make a mental note of where the court of women is.[3] On the roof there are colonnades that encircle the court where women stand above and the men stand below. In the center of the court are four large menorahs (raised on bases 50 yards high) each with seven lights. The lights are so strong they would light up all of Jerusalem.[4] Can you picture the scene?

Remember how I told you that this feast was the most joyous? Well, this scene helps you picture why. Torch dancers, singing, harps, flutes, trumpets. It's all there.

I'm sure during Jesus' day it was quite the sight to behold.[5]

This particular scene happens every night of the feast. The Feast of Tabernacles, like the others the Jewish people celebrated, takes into account the past, present, and future. The light symbolized not only what God had done in the past (pillar of fire/light that led the Israelites through the wilderness) but also pointed forward to what God was going to do, specifically through the coming Messiah. In between the past deliverance and the future hope—in the present—they celebrated.

Enter Jesus.

Let's pick up during what might have been the time of the torch dance at the end of the night.

READ JOHN 8:12-20.

> Verse 12 lists two promises that the Light of the world brings. List them here just so we have them handy:
>
> 1.
>
> 2.

Jesus makes this statement within the context of the Feast of Tabernacles. When Jesus says He is the light, He is essentially saying that He came to put an end to the meaning of the traditions by fulfilling their intent. Jesus in every way fulfills and surpasses every image and symbol of light that came before Him.

It's easy for us to read quickly through verses and sometimes miss important words or phrases. For instance, in John 8:12, Jesus says, "Whoever *follows* me." What is the significance of this word usage? As we talked about earlier, this feast was a celebration as the people of Israel recalled the goodness of God who led them out of slavery in Egypt. The Israelites literally "followed" a pillar of fire, the light of the Lord, through the perilous wilderness into the promised land. Now, as we follow Jesus we are led out of our wilderness and darkness into His light—the light of life.

Jesus said that once we have the light we will not walk in darkness. But, He did not say that He would take the darkness away. You and I both know we live in a dark world that needs all the light it can get. That's why we must follow where the Light leads.

The Temple

1. Holy of Holies
2. Holy Place
3. Veil
4. Altar of Incense
5. Table of Shewbread
6. Seven-branched Lampstand
7. Court of Priests
8. Court of Israel (men)
9. Altar of Burnt Offerings
10. Animal Preparation Area
11. East Gate
12. Court of Women
13. Women's Balconies

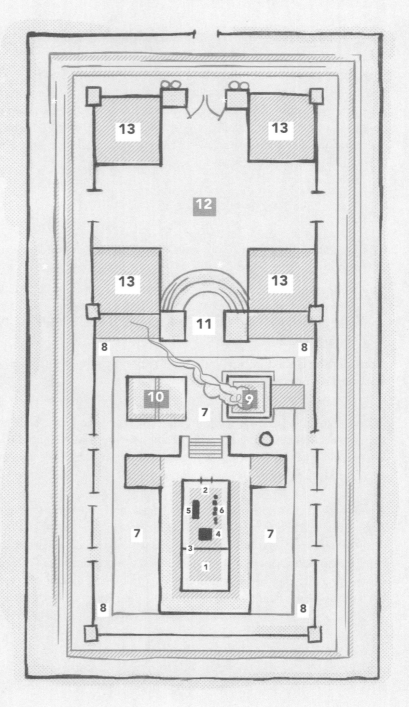

What are some examples from your life right now of walking in the light where Jesus is leading you? How have you seen others walk in the light?

It seems like more and more people are turning away from God and following after their own way. It can be easy to get so focused on the darkness around us that we never address the darkness in us. Any place we are afraid of being exposed is evidence of possible darkness in us.

Let's be honest here for a minute. In what areas of your life do you feel like you are in darkness?

Well-known preacher Charles Spurgeon said, "Dear friend, if you are afraid of light, be suspicious of yourself, for it is deceit that dreads detection."[6] If you don't stop and recognize potential areas of darkness in your life you may just keep living there—unaware. Even more dangerous is hiding from the light and growing accustomed to the darkness, only to be deceived by its momentary pleasure.

Consider the breakthrough you might experience by determining to address the dark and sinful places in your life.

EXPOSING			EXPERIENCING		
sin	what's holding me back	chains	light	forgiveness	freedom
The darkness where we believe the lie that what we are doing outside of God's truth isn't that big of a deal. Or the lie that it would be impossible for us to escape this sin.	Recognizing that we are getting some longing or need met outside God's will and best plans for us.	What we thought would free us from pain and loneliness is actually the very sin that binds us and strips us from our freedom in Christ.	God's revelation that there's a better way. He can help us. Restore our hope. And heal the hurt. We just have to engage with and step into the light of His truth. Lies flee in the presence of truth.	Experience a marked time where you ask God for forgiveness. Be specific. And then pray, "God, I receive Your forgiveness."	John 8:32, "Then you will know the truth, and the truth will set you free." Say, "I am free to experience peace and restoration in this situation where the lies are dismissed and truth is applied."

How did this progression chart help you look at your situation a little bit differently?

READ JOHN 3:19-21.

What did the people love? And why?

Sometimes as we read Scripture, we need to intentionally pause and ask why. If we are honest, as we read John 3:19-21 we can see ourselves. There is a certain sense of comfort when we sin in the darkness. The comfort of feeling like our deeds are masked by the darkness. The comfort that we won't be exposed so we can continue to enjoy the fleeting pleasures of sin. Ultimately, it's always more comfortable to sin in darkness due to the false sense that what we do is private and unknown; it's hidden. The good news is that there is hope for us. Jesus is our hope. He is the light that illuminates the darkness for our good and His glory. It's scary to consider that even if I have the light I am still prone to walk in darkness. What an incredible reminder to know that Christ not only brings light, but He also brings deliverance from the darkness.

> He has delivered us from the domain of darkness and transferred us to the kingdom of his beloved Son, in whom we have redemption, the forgiveness of sins.
>
> COLOSSIANS 1:13-14, ESV

The great news is that Christ is in the business of bringing the light of Himself into dark places, and for that I am thankful.

One more flashback to the feast celebration. Jesus watched the Jewish leaders light the feast lamps each night, but the light didn't transform anybody. They were just as blind as ever. Some commentators suggest that Jesus actually uttered the words "I AM the light of the world" at the end of the feast after all the lights have been blown out by the priests. What a picture of Jesus in the middle of the darkness!

And He's standing in the midst of my darkness and yours as well. We all have places in our life where we've refused Jesus and shut out His light. Remember, Jesus isn't trying to expose you to put shame on you. He's trying to expose the sin that has its chains around you. His light not only helps us get free but see where to walk from here.

In your darkness and in mine—whatever and wherever it might be—let Jesus shine His bright light because He is the Light. The world has no other light than Him. It is Jesus or darkness; there is no third alternative. If you see or notice light in the world, it is Jesus. Notice the light today and invite Him into any darkness that may be in or around you. He wants to come and fill it.

Jesus isn't trying to expose you to put shame on you. He's trying to expose the sin that has its chains around you.

LIGHT WORD STUDY

We are going to spend today's lesson focusing in on several key passages in the Bible where we see the word *light*. And we will start all the way back at the very beginning.

READ GENESIS 1:1-5.

What was the first thing God spoke into existence?

How was this light created?

In Genesis 1:2 we find that the world was in utter chaos, void, without form, and engulfed in darkness. God's first recorded action is seen as He makes a declarative statement, "Let there be light" (v. 3). And just as He spoke it, it was!

Yes, before all of creation could come into existence, God determined that light needed to be present and that it was necessary to have a separation between the light and darkness (Gen. 1:4b).

As we begin to see the rest of creation take form, it's important to note how light sustains each part of it. Take a moment and consider the function and purpose of light in creation:

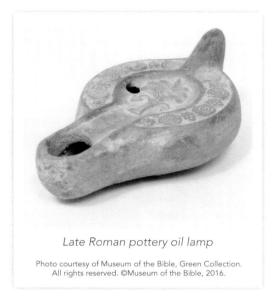

Late Roman pottery oil lamp

- It dispels darkness revealing what is hidden;

- It illuminates what is beautiful;

- It gives warmth;

- It causes growth;

- It literally sustains life.

In the same way that light is active in creation, the light of God is not a passive experience. We don't just simply sit back and gaze at the beauty of God; we also experience and respond to the light of Christ!

Light is not only at the very beginning of Genesis; it's at the very beginning of John as well. Thousands of years after the creation of light, the actual Light came into the world in the form of Jesus to rescue us from ultimate darkness.

READ JOHN 1:1-5.

Write down what you see and learn about light in this passage.

Make no mistake—darkness is trying to overcome the light. There is a reason it feels like we are in a battle every day.

READ 2 CORINTHIANS 11:14.

How does Satan disguise himself?

Knowledge is power. If we can recognize Satan for who he is when he tries to show up in our lives as light, then we can call him out on it and reach for the true light of Jesus.

We love getting on social media to connect with people but can't help feeling a little "off" as we compare our lives to the pictures we see others posting. Darkness disguised as light.

Or we really want to see that movie that all our friends are talking about. But, that movie affects us in more ways than we know. Darkness disguised as light.

Can you think of areas in your life where darkness is disguised as light?

So, how do we tell the difference? If something looks like light, how can we know if it is really light or if it is counterfeit light? Psalm 119:105 says, "Your word is a lamp for my feet, a light on my path," and then later in that same chapter we see: "The unfolding of your words gives light; it gives understanding to the simple" (Ps. 119:130).

To tell if something is truly the light we must hold it up to the light of God's Word.

What does it mean to hold something up to God's Word?

Let's take a look at what true light brings. Look up the Scripture listed below and write what His light brings in each scenario.

VERSE	HIS LIGHT BRINGS
2 Corinthians 4:6	knowledge of God's glory
Psalm 119:130	giveth Understanding
Isaiah 60:19-20	
John 3:19-21	
1 John 1:5-7	
James 1:17	

What decision or situation are you facing right now where you need some guidance? How can holding it up to God's Word and what we just learned about light and darkness help you in that situation?

Please keep testing your decisions against Scripture. Our world is telling us that we don't need God's Word, that the Bible is out of date. It's certainly not popular. So, the tendency is to let it fall by the wayside and simply go with what we feel is right. That kind of thinking is a dangerous lie from Satan. Any time you feel it may be easier to go it on your own and not bring a decision back to God's Word, recognize that thinking for what it is—a lie from Satan. The Word of God is our handbook for living. Keep it close and use it as a light unto your path every day.

The Word of God is our handbook for living.

We started this theme of light today in Genesis and we will end today's lesson, appropriately, in the last chapter of our Bible.

READ REVELATION 22:1-5.

What creation themes did you see in these verses?

According to this passage, why will we no longer need the light of the lamp or the light of the sun?

Finally, in the end, Jesus will become the only true light we will need. God truly weaves His Word together in such a beautiful way. I pray we may all see a glimpse of the light of Jesus today and ask Him to give us more and more of that light as we look forward to the day Revelation describes.

HEALING THE MAN BORN BLIND

Do you ever have little places of discouragement that tangle around your heart? You know in the bigger picture of life things are good, but there's this little dark place. A little black hole. That sometimes doesn't feel little. It hangs like a cloud—blocking the sun, casting shadows.

Maybe it's an argument you and your husband have had one too many times. Your relationship is good, but this one topic feels like a black hole. Maybe it's an issue with one of your kids. You have an amazing child, but there is this one behavioral tendency that baffles you, embarrasses you, and causes you to fear. It feels like a black hole. Maybe it's a recurring frustration with a friend. She's great, but there's this one part of your friendship that darkens the collective good. And you can't figure out how to address it. Now it's happening with more frequency, and it feels like a black hole.

Last night I was up again praying and crying out to God to help me better process some of the hard situations in my life.

I asked God to shed some of His light on what I'm struggling through so I don't get lost in the darkness of confusion. His voice wasn't loud or definitive. Just a slight shift of my thoughts to be in line with truth and I knew light was defeating my darkness.

LOOK AT ALL THE PRAYERS THAT HAVE BEEN ANSWERED WITH THIS SITUATION. Small changes. The big, grand finale I keep hoping for hasn't yet come. But might I notice the beautiful symphony of hopeful notes in the in-between?

LOOK AT THE STRENGTH I'M GAINING IN THE PROCESS. Every time I turn to God and ask for Him to shed light on my situation, I'm trading a little of my struggle for a bit of His strength.

LOOK AT THE REALITY THAT A BLACK HOLE ISN'T A BLACK WHOLE. The whole isn't all bad. Yes, there are some issues to address and some tensions to manage, but I can't let Satan use this frustration to darken my outlook.

Remember what we learned about Jesus in John 8? He is the Light of the world!

Ask Jesus to shed His light on your situation today. Look at this from Jesus' perspective. Use truth to do something positive in this area today. Invest the time to make a little imperfect progress right there in the dark place. It won't be so dark with a little Light cast upon it.

In John 9, we see Jesus reiterate the claim that He is the Light of the world and put action to it by healing the man born blind.

READ THIS ACCOUNT IN JOHN 9:1-12.

Why did the disciples think this man was blind (v.2)?

What did Jesus say was the real reason (v.3)?

We so often want to know why. I know I do. If we can figure out the why then life makes a little bit more sense, especially if there is pain or suffering. Even if we don't ask, "Why?" out loud, it is usually the first question we ask in our hearts. The disciples were looking for someone to blame for this unfortunate situation. If they could only figure out the reason why, then the hurt of this man would be more tolerable.

I really hope the disciples asked more than just this one question as they passed by this man. I hope they asked questions like, "How can we help this man?" Perhaps they did and we just don't have it recorded—we can't know for sure, but I'm hopeful. I'm hopeful that the disciples weren't themselves blind to the need right there in front of them. What we do know, though, is that the disciples wanted to use this man as a theology lesson. And Jesus took them up on that offer.

Being blind in Jesus' time was often seen as a statement about the sin in your life. So, you probably didn't have a whole lot of help from people. In their eyes, you were not only blind—you were assumed to be a sinner whom God was punishing. Jesus turns this thinking on its head and tells the disciples that the reason this man is blind is so that we can all witness God's amazing power.

Put yourself in the shoes of this blind man. Without the ability to see, he has to rely on secondhand information for almost everything. There is a certain sense of frustration when someone tries to explain an incredible scene, sight, or experience. It is one thing to sit passively and listen to a firsthand account of an experience. It is something completely different to actually have that experience.

We don't have to be physically blind to only see darkness.

The Pharisees were in this same camp. They knew all about the prophesied Messiah. But when Jesus came on the scene they couldn't see that He was the One. They knew all the right answers, but didn't make the right choice.

Do you have someone like that in your life? Or, do you see glimpses of this tendency in your own life? Write a prayer for that situation.

The Pool of Siloam

Jesus gave the blind man instructions on what to do to be healed. He wasn't healed right there. The blind man had to obey. Don't miss that part. Jesus is the Light and He wants to bring healing to us, but sometimes that means a step of obedience on our part.

> Is there a situation in your life where you heard clearly from the Lord that you should take some kind of action, but you haven't followed through yet? If so, record some of that situation here. Are there steps you need to take now to follow through on this?

I so want spiritual sight in my life, don't you? I want to be able to approach a situation in my life that might look hopeless and see the spiritual potential. I want to read the Bible and see clearly what God wants to say to me. I want to know how to react to situations in the way that honors Christ.

I think the only way we get that spiritual sight is to continually ask God for it. He is the One who can illuminate the dark places for us. So we must ask. And we must ask regularly.

Well, are you wondering what happened to the man born blind? What becomes of him? In John 9:13-34, we see the Pharisees questioning the blind man and his parents. The Pharisees still did not believe even though they saw the evidence of the healing as they were speaking to this man. Then the Pharisees threw the once-blind man out because they didn't like what he had to say about Jesus. Let's pick up there.

He is the One who can illuminate the dark places for us.

READ THE END OF THE STORY IN JOHN 9:35-41.

This is both a beautiful and sad ending to the story. The man who was blind began to follow after Jesus, and the Pharisees who could physically see the world clearly were still blind to the Savior standing in front of them. Please know it is possible for Jesus to be in our midst and for us to still have a Pharisee heart.

This story reminds me of a well-loved hymn. The lyrics to "Amazing Grace" are probably very familiar to you.

Amazing grace! How sweet the sound
That saved a wretch like me!
I once was lost, but now am found;
Was blind, but now I see.[7]

The man who penned this most famous hymn has an interesting story. John Newton lived in England during the 1700s. When he was young he was taught the gospel and was active in church for a time, but then turned away from it in his young adult years. In fact, he became a slave trader who turned his back on his faith. He not only neglected his faith, but also directly opposed it, mocking others who showed theirs and denouncing God as a myth.

Then, in 1748, while he was on board the ship The Greyhound, a storm came and John almost died. God got his attention that day, and John began to take steps toward Christ. He would eventually become a pastor and sought hard after those with a "hard heart." He was a unique preacher for the time in that he didn't shy away from sharing about his own past and present struggles in the faith. Newton's life and writing shows how captivated he was by the amazing grace of God. Shortly before his death, in one of his last messages he proclaimed, "My memory is nearly gone, but I remember two things: That I am a great sinner and that Christ is a great Savior!"[8]

I love this story because it reminds me that my story isn't over yet and neither is yours.

God, we need Your light. Light defeats darkness every time. I might not have all the answers to my struggles right now but I am seeing more hope than ever. Jesus is my light. And because of Him even my darkest of nights aren't so daunting and confusing. Oh Jesus, bring Your light and with You I am comforted.

OPTIONAL
READ JOHN 5–9.

Good questions to ask as you read are:
What does this passage teach me about God?

_____

_____

_____

_____

_____

_____

_____

_____

_____

_____

_____

What does this passage teach me about myself?

_____

_____

_____

_____

_____

_____

_____

_____

_____

_____

_____

_____

What do I need to do as a result of reading this passage?

As you read John today, see which of these attributes of God are exemplified and write any thoughts you have about them.

Compassionate	Good	Faithful	Holy	Patient	Wise
Generous	Loving	Just	True	All-Knowing	
All-Powerful	Eternal	Gracious	Merciful	Faithful	

Video Session 3

WATCH VIDEO SESSION 3 AND RECORD YOUR NOTES BELOW.

Scripture in this video session:
John 4:3-43 • Gen. 37:24 • Jer. 38:6 • Jer. 2:13 • Rev. 22:16-17

Pray list
 Sandy
Andrew
 Daniel
 Brad
Missy + Jim
 Justin + Mandy
  Debbie + Pat
Casey Creek Erick
 Brett Brock

Video sessions available for purchase
at www.lifeway.com/findingIAM

VIDEO GROUP DISCUSSION QUESTIONS

After watching the video, discuss the following questions in your group.

1. What do you think the Samaritan woman was thirsting for?

   Love friends exception Caring

2. Jesus purposely went through Samaria so He could encounter this woman. How does this comfort you?

3. How does the Samaritan woman's unquenchable thirst for more of something compare to the things we thirst for today?

4. What is an example of a broken cistern that you or someone you know has gone to in order to draw water, but that water didn't satisfy?

5. This Samaritan woman had a thirst, found Jesus as the source of living water, and then became a light to her world. How do you see the same progression happen today?

5 m Scripture Pray

Book of John

Gate

———

Shepherd

VERY TRULY I TELL YOU, I AM THE GATE FOR THE SHEEP.

JOHN 10:7

I AM THE GOOD SHEPHERD.

JOHN 10:11

#FINDINGIAM

A LOOK AT SHEEP

Sheep are mentioned in the Bible over 300 times—more than any other animal.[1] That's fascinating, isn't it? Sometimes I wish we knew more about sheep than most of us living in the modern age do. Unless you have a farming background you likely don't know a whole lot about this particular animal. I actually learned a lot about sheep when I was in Israel. Let's note a few characteristics of sheep.

- **Sheep are defenseless animals.**
- **Sheep are prone to go astray.**
- **Sheep have poor eyesight.**
- **Sheep tend to follow other sheep without thinking.**
- **Sheep are stubborn.**

In fact, there are some accounts of sheep actually getting stuck on their backs and even dying because they were unable to get back on their feet! Needless to say, we can view sheep as being utterly helpless.

I don't know about you, but I think I may be catching on to why we are referred to as sheep.

Let's dive in today to Luke 15. In this passage Jesus talks about a sheep that is lost.

TAKE A MOMENT AND READ LUKE 15:1-7.

In what setting is Jesus telling this story? And to whom is He telling the story?

Does anyone else besides me scratch their heads when they read this story? If I were a shepherd, I have a feeling I would pat myself on the back if I got home with 99 percent of my sheep, right? I mean, really, look back at the characteristics of sheep—prone to go astray, follow other sheep without thinking, poor eyesight. It would probably be a miracle that I only lost one sheep and not more!

Have you ever wondered how that one sheep got lost? Do you think he was willfully disobedient? Did he think, *Man, I don't like the way this shepherd is leading us; he can't be trusted so I'm out of here.* No, I don't think that was how he got lost. I think it went more like this.

He started eating some grass and while eating the grass thought, *Wow, this grass is pretty good.* The pleasure of immediately satisfying his desire probably got him off track, and he found himself not paying attention to the other sheep around him. And then all of a sudden he looked up, and all the other sheep were nowhere to be found. He probably didn't have any idea he was off track. He may have been out of sync with the others for a while but had no idea.

I have a feeling that's how we all get lost sometimes. We find ourselves a little discouraged or distracted, and we just start to subtly slide away. We start sitting on the back row. We miss a few weeks of church. We don't sign up for the next small group study. We make excuses, and then we find an exit. A way out. We take a step, then another step, and then before long we look up and wonder, *How in the world did I get here?* And, *where are all the other sheep?*

I know. I've been there.

Recently, I had a conversation with a good friend about the source of the sorrow I wrote about in Week 1. Last year she knew I was going through a really hard time. She would find various ways to try and address it, bring it out of me, get me to tell her something, anything. She could feel something was wrong but was confused why I wouldn't talk to her about it. Worst of all, she knew if I wouldn't talk to her about it, I wouldn't be talking to anyone about it.

She could feel me slipping away from deep conversations, making everything way more shallow than it ever should be between us. I would talk about kids and work and everyday challenges, but the minute she tried to step into deep waters with me I pulled away. And I pulled back. I would text instead of call. I would always have an excuse why we couldn't connect.

It wasn't because I didn't want to talk to her about my sorrow. It was because I felt if I admitted to her how disillusioned I was that God wasn't answering the prayer I've prayed for years, it would give God even more reason to never answer it. That's not true; I see that now. But the more alone we get with lies, the more confused we become.

Then time did what it always does; it marched on. One month turned into 2, 3, 4, 10, 11. It's unbelievable how quickly someone can become completely isolated when they pull away from intimate relationships. I was surrounded by people on the outside but completely alone on the inside.

Has this ever happened to you? Describe a time you isolated yourself, believing lies about the truth of God.

And that's where the enemy wants us—alone. Alone with our own tangled thoughts. Alone with his whispered lies that start to sound more and more like truths. Separated from the very people who could speak courage into our deep places flirting with discouragement and defeat. Separated from friends who could let us stand on their faith when our own gets a little shaky.

The enemy knows if he can isolate us, he can intimidate us. Confuse us. Deceive us. And ultimately, make us believe that the safer paths in life are ones apart from God and our friends who serve God.

Suddenly, one day I woke up and felt more alone than I'd ever felt in my life. I kept smiling and saying things like "I'm fine. Everything is good. Doing well." But while I was smiling on the outside, I was screaming on the inside, *God where are You?*

Probably a better question would have been, *God, where have I wandered off to?*

Then one day I was riding in the car with a girl I barely knew. She kept asking me questions and in an effort to fill what would have otherwise felt like an awkward silence, I gave her answers. My replies were nothing but an inch deep. Shallow. Non-revealing. Typical and tired answers hoping to satisfy her into a hush. Then suddenly she volunteered what she'd been learning about prayer. She got my attention with descriptions of her prayer life like: Flat. Disengaged. Distant. Something stirred deep inside me. I pursed my lips together so the words "me, too" didn't escape. Otherwise, I feared the questions about me would start up again. Then a word tumbled from her mouth with great enthusiasm, "confession." Confession had been the key to a deeper reconnection with God.

Come near to God and he will come near to you.

JAMES 4:8

Honestly, I'd been so focused on my desires, my suggestions, and my strategies for fixing things I'd lost sight of my Good Shepherd with a good plan. After getting out of the car, I silently prayed, "God, I confess I've not been trusting You to lead me. I've been so focused on my desperation that I couldn't hear Your revelation, 'Lysa, I am good. And my plan is good. Trust me. Follow me. And reconnect with your friend who can speak my good truth over you and your struggles.'"

James 4:8 says, "Come near to God and he will come near to you." God was there.

He'd pressed past my resistance. He crossed the borders of my trust issues. He climbed the hills of my heartbreaks. He came to bring me back. He came to remind me I can't do life alone.

He came for me. He heard my cries. He cared.

That realization rattled me out of the fog of lies clouding my path. After that, I didn't just get deeply honest with my one friend I had pushed away. I circled up with several trusted companions and let truth build bridges to keep us connected in the midst of the disappointments and heartbreaks we were all facing.

I wonder if it is time to take an inventory of the direction you are headed and the small decision you've made that has led to another step away. Have you checked your course lately? Have you been looking for the Shepherd and His leading? Do you have your fellow sheep around you?

Pause a moment and take inventory by answering the questions above.

Sometimes our wandering can be complex and multifaceted. Maybe you have wandered off course not even realizing it. It was a slow and steady process that left you alone and stranded. Maybe it's intentional. You may have found pleasure in something that captivated you and drew you off course. Sadly, even good things can often turn into idols in our lives that get us isolated and alone. If you have wandered, you are not alone; it happens to the best of us. Take a moment and think about the lost sheep. At some point the sheep realized all the other sheep were gone. What would the sheep do? I think instinct would be to listen for the familiar voice of the shepherd.

May this parable be a reminder to us that in the midst of our wilderness the Good Shepherd is pursuing us, calling out to us, bringing us back to the fold, and willing to take back the lead in the journey. We just have to pray something simple like this, "Jesus, I recognize I have strayed and I am willing to turn from the choices that got me off course. I need help. I need Your guidance. Hold me close. Lead me. Guide me."

I'm thankful that the Good Shepherd comes and finds us no matter how we get lost or how far we wander—whether it's through willful disobedience or through just taking one bad step at a time until we are way off course.

Okay, go back and recall with me. Who was Jesus speaking to in this parable again? And what were the Pharisees angry with Jesus about?

The crowd consisted of the tax collectors and sinners (lost sheep) and the Pharisees (the 99 righteous ones who thought they didn't need to repent). I can imagine why the Pharisees were angry. They had devoted themselves to moralistic living. They had followed the law obsessively. From their perspective they were above reproach and they desperately wanted the accolades that came with this right living. Jesus shattered their way of thinking. Jesus not only clearly answered their question; He also exposed their sin and selfish nature. Jesus has come for the lost sheep, and there is great rejoicing in heaven over sinners who repent and turn from their ways.

SHEEP GATE

DAY 2

SHEEP GATE

Today we find ourselves learning from two distinct instances in Jesus' ministry, yet they are very much connected. In John 9, we read about Jesus healing the man who was born blind. In that instance of healing, Jesus proves in a tangible way that He is Light of the world. However, "the Jews," as John called them (John 10:19; the religious leaders), seem to be quarreling constantly with Jesus and trying to capture Him because the I AM statements He claims are equating Him with God.

In John 10, we see Jesus introduce another I AM statement to the hostile crowd.

READ JOHN 10:1-10, BUT PAY SPECIAL ATTENTION TO THE FIRST VERSE.

> John 10:1 has a distinct tone. How would you describe Jesus' state of mind as He goes from chapter 9 to chapter 10?

Jesus may not be angry in this verse, but He certainly seems to be making a point by how He speaks of the thief and bandit. Perhaps the thief and the bandit are still in His midst hearing these words as He is about to share with them yet another I AM statement.

Before we go any further, let's do a little digging to find out more about shepherds in this time period and place.

The setting here is a small Jewish village. Most families owned a few sheep and would partner together with other families so they could hire a shepherd to care for their sheep. Overnight the sheep were placed in roughly constructed round stone-walled enclosures. The top of the wall was covered with thorns to keep the wild animals out. Inside the enclosure the sheep were safe so long as the entrance was secured by the shepherd. He slept across the entrance as there was no door.[2]

It would be good to remind ourselves why the sheep are in this enclosure. The sheep are prone to wander and cause self harm. The only way to keep them safe from themselves and wild predators—like wolves—was to keep them in this enclosure.

How did the sheep know to follow the shepherd (see vv. 3-5)?

That voice. The sheep had come to know it well.

Often times, when we read Scripture, we process its meaning through the filter of what we know and experience in our everyday lives. Because we don't live in a middle eastern country during biblical times, we simply don't recognize some of the important details in God's Word that the people of that day would have immediately identified with. I really believe one of the most powerful things we can do to help us more fully understand the Bible is to learn about the cultural context it was written in. Then we can compare that knowledge to the way we think about things based on our own experiences and culture today. This helps give you an accurate picture of how a scenario would have played out in biblical times. It also helps you identify deeper meanings surrounding particular passages.

Shepherding is a perfect example of how our modern understanding of something could pull us away from grasping all that God wants us to embrace in His Word.

In some cultures today, shepherding includes using a herding dog and gates or physical structures as the main methods to confine sheep. The way to get sheep to move is to send the dog out and "herd" them. Essentially, the herding dog runs around the sheep to cause them to panic and run towards a specific direction. It's common for the dogs to nip at the feet or body of the sheep in order to get them to move. In this method of shepherding, the way to get sheep to move and obey is through panic and pain.

However, if you had been in Israel during the time of Jesus, you would have witnessed a much different scene. There weren't any pain tactics to keep the sheep on the right path. In fact, the shepherd took every measure to make sure each of his sheep was safe and without blemish. He would often put himself in danger simply to protect his flock. In this concept of shepherding, the way to care for the sheep was through tenderness, trust, and nurturing.

> How does understanding this cultural difference change the way you view Scripture referring to God and Jesus as our Shepherd?

I love knowing how the shepherds cared for their sheep, and, as a result, how the sheep learned to trust and hear the voice of the beloved shepherd.

Day after day the sheep heard the voice of their shepherd. Day after day his voice led them, provided for them, and kept them from harm. They ignored any other voice that tried to lead them astray because they didn't know or trust it. In fact, there were probably multiple flocks within the sheep gate. How did they separate the sheep? It was simple, the shepherd's voice. The sheep knew the voice of their shepherd, and when he called they would respond and follow.

What a beautiful illustration of our own relationship with God. I often wish I could audibly hear the voice of God. I feel this way when it comes to big decisions. I felt this way in my time of sorrow. But I also wish I could hear Him audibly in the mundane parts of life when my greatest desire is just to have Him lead and reassure me that I'm on the right path.

However, even though I've never heard the audible voice of God, I can still feel His direction and sense His presence when I seek Him. I know the will of God when I read and pray the Word of God.

> What about you? Where and how do you hear God's voice in your life?

KEYS TO HEARING GOD'S VOICE:

1. **SCRIPTURE:** God speaks to us primarily through His Word. If we are going to God's Word daily to hear from Him, He will speak.

2. **PEACE OF GOD:** Are you wondering about a specific decision or action in your life? Watch for the peace of God. The Holy Spirit often works through giving us peace about a situation. Watch and pay attention for that peace and ask if that is God's voice talking to you.

3. **GODLY COUNSEL:** God speaks to us through godly people. If we are seeking to hear from the Lord on something, we can bring it to people who are a little bit older and wiser in the faith and let them help us think it through. God uses other believers in our lives to either confirm something or steer us in a different direction.

4. **LISTEN:** If we really want to hear from God we need to set aside time to listen. Sometimes God speaks through a still, small voice and if we are moving too quickly we could miss it.

5. **OBEY:** We need to be sure to obey what God told us to do last time before we can expect to hear from Him again.

Would you add any others to this list?

Which key could you work on implementing in your life this week? Write out a plan to do so.

If you are in relationship with God and hear from Him on a regular basis, please don't take that for granted. For those of us who may not hear from Him as much as we'd like, I thought it might be good for us to review barriers that might be keeping us from hearing. Note that this is not an exhaustive list and these are not failsafe measures, but rather points to ponder as we explore hearing the voice of our Shepherd.

BARRIERS TO HEARING GOD'S VOICE:

1. **NOT SETTING ASIDE TIME:** God wants to speak to us, but if we are too busy to hear from Him we will certainly miss the important things He is trying to teach us.

2. **PRIDE:** Sometimes thinking we already know best cuts us off from humbling ourselves to hear from our Creator.

3. **UNCONFESSED SIN:** Sin that remains hidden in our hearts is truly a block from hearing from God. Search yourself to see if you need to confess something to God, and I bet you'll start to hear from Him more often.

4. **BITTERNESS AND RESENTMENT:** Our hearts get hard sometimes for many different reasons. Pray that the Lord would soften your heart to hear from Him in a deeper way.

5. **FEAR:** Sometimes we don't want to hear God's voice because we are afraid of what He may ask of us. So, we stop hearing all together.

   Would you add any others to this list?

   Which barrier is most relevant to you right now? Stop and ask God to remove that barrier as you continue in your study.

You may go through seasons where God seems silent in an area of your life. Don't let that discourage you. You are not alone. In that type of season, remember that your relationship with God is the most important. Keep trusting Him. Keep praying. Keep watching for Him. And remember, God's Word is Him speaking to us in written form—always available, and never silent.

One of my favorite places to turn in Scripture when my heart is desperate to hear from God is to the Book of Isaiah. Did you know there are seven references to "I AM" in Isaiah as well? These are beautifully bold and deeply reassuring to my heart.

Notice these revelations of God are all stated with "I am he." Read these passages in Isaiah and write down words from each that personally stir your heart. God is speaking to You through His Word.

Isaiah 41:4

Isaiah 43:10

Isaiah 43:13

Isaiah 43:25

Isaiah 46:4

Isaiah 48:12

Isaiah 51:12

What reassuring truths about God stood out to you from these verses?

Think about these Scriptures in the context of Jesus fulfilling the prophecies of Isaiah by being our Shepherd and Sheep Gate. He is our protector, our provider, our portion, and our pathway. He is everything we need and so perfectly capable of filling in the gaps of our wants as well. We must let these truths seep deep into the longings of our soul. Otherwise lies are prone to creep into this place of desire.

Remember yesterday when I said the more alone we get with lies, the more confused we become? It's so important that we stay in the presence of truth and actively keep the lies of the enemy out of our minds. Because as a woman thinks, so she eventually acts. I saw this happen a few years ago when I watched a friend make choices that led to complete financial ruin and broken relationships.

She was a strong Christian woman who loved her family and valued honesty. But somewhere along the line she began to compare her life with what others had and rationalized purchases she really couldn't afford. Her heart played tricks on her mind and the justifications for letting things go just a little further soon led her to a very dangerous place. She was spending much more than she could repay and kept it hidden from her husband.

In a moment of desperation, she came to me one day and told me what was going on. As she described how she got pulled into this place, I found myself being challenged by the realization of how subtly this had happened. She hadn't planned on being deceptive and placing her family in financial hardship. As a matter of fact, she'd always prided herself on being a woman of strong conviction and responsibility. But as she saw others living the life she wanted, she began taking matters into her own hands to make it happen for her.

It starts off simple enough—entertaining a few thoughts of jealousy and comparison, making an extra online purchase, bending the monthly budget just a bit past what you and your husband had agreed on, opening a secret credit card, or one of a thousand other things that seem small yet aren't. And bit by bit she started pulling away from what she knew to be right.

Our thoughts are so powerful. We must make them work for us instead of against us.

The time to prevent a financial crisis, a complete breakdown, or a distant relationship from God is before it ever starts. We must never assume *it could never happen to me*. We are all just a few poor choices away from doing things we never thought we would. Especially when our hearts are in a vulnerable place of longing for something that God hasn't yet provided. It may not be buying things you can't afford right now. There are many ways our hearts can be led away from God. We are either holding fast to God's promise or being lured by a compromise. And isn't it interesting that the word *promise* is right there in the midst of that word *com(promise)*? Jesus warned His disciples in Matthew 26:41, "Watch and pray so that you will not fall into temptation. The spirit is willing, but the flesh is weak."

The Life Application NIV Bible commentary says, "Jesus used Peter's drowsiness to warn him to be spiritually vigilant against the temptation he would soon face. The way to overcome temptation is to stay alert and to pray. This means being aware of the possibilities of temptation, sensitive to the subtleties, and morally resolved to fight courageously."[3]

STAY ALERT: I now realize that I need to be aware that I am just as prone to this temptation as anyone.

SENSITIVE TO THE SUBTLETIES: I will have to be honest with myself that temptations do exist.

MORALLY RESOLVED: I must park my mind on the truth found in God's Word.

My friend did the hardest but wisest thing she could have done in telling me about her situation. It helped her to see she needed to flee from the lies she'd been believing and have someone else hold her accountable. It brought her back to a place where she could surrender her thoughts under God's truth.

You may not be in the same situation as my friend, but chances are, Satan wants you to go down a similar road of self-destructive behavior.

> If you sense yourself headed down a destructive path, take action now to tell someone. If you aren't in that situation currently, what are some ways you can take steps now to not go down that path? List some ideas here and put them into practice.

It can be so dangerous when we stop listening for God's voice or when we believe the lie that He is silent in our situation. The sheep recognize the shepherd's voice because they know him. He is not a stranger to them. They have seen that they can trust him and therefore they follow him. If we want to hear God's voice, we have to know Him. We have to trust Him. And we also have to recognize what is not His voice so we can turn away from the lies and the "strangers."

The most important thing is tuning our heart to hear God's voice and follow Him. Lord Jesus, may it be so.

So we end our lesson with the visual of Jesus as the Sheep Gate.

LOOK BACK AT JOHN 10:9-10.

What three things does Jesus promise about the sheep in this verse?

While the sheep find their salvation in the form of safe passage and ready pasture, the believer finds her salvation through the perfect shepherding and care of God.

What do you think it means for us to "come in and go out, and find pasture"?

What can we learn from the fact that Jesus is claiming that He is the literal Sheep Gate?

Remember during Week 1 where I talked about the desperation I sometimes feel because of a longing in my heart not yet met? I have to invite my Shepherd's voice of truth into this place of my heart especially. He must be the gate that keeps the enemy's thoughts and temptations from entering this vulnerable place inside me.

Throughout the course of human history there has always been a claim for satisfaction, pleasure, and self-fulfillment from things other than Jesus. The claims are endless when it comes to alternative paths to abundant life. When Jesus makes this declarative statement that He is the Sheep Gate, He confirms that the only way to salvation is through Him. Consider this bold claim. Jesus is not just an alternative or better way, He is the only way to the Father. Therefore, Jesus is the only way to the Father's best plans for me.

The abundant and good life that Christ offers is gained simply through Him. Thank Jesus for being your Sheep Gate and be on the alert to hear and respond to His voice.

Jesus is not just an alternative or better way, He is the only way to the Father.

A LOOK AT SHEPHERDS

Now that we know a little more about sheep and the sheep gate, let's turn our full attention to the shepherd. We find God using and interacting with shepherds all throughout the Bible.

It doesn't take us long in the Scriptures to get to the first shepherd.

READ GENESIS 4:1-9.

Who was the first shepherd mentioned in the Bible?

What word describes the animals Abel brought to sacrifice to the Lord in verse 4?

The Bible does not give us insight into why God preferred Abel's sacrifice here in Genesis. Cain brought an offering of fruit from the ground, and Abel brought the firstborn of his livestock, specifically their fat portions. We do know that in Israel the "fat portions" were considered to be the most valuable and best portions. It cost Abel something to bring the finest that he had and give it to the Lord (2 Sam. 24:24). What a powerful reminder for us to consider the type of "sacrifice" that we bring to the Lord!

The famous Hall of Faith in Hebrews 11 lists hero in the faith after hero in the faith. It is here we learn more about the sacrifices of the two brothers.

> Notice with me and record the first person mentioned (Heb. 11:4).
>
> *ABEL*
>
> Why was his sacrifice acceptable, according to this passage?

I am challenged to recognize how important it is to bring my offering to the Lord first and in faith. But also, I want to give God my first thoughts in faith every day. I want to turn to Him first in faith as I'm thinking about the cry of my heart as well. He wants to be first and He wants me to come to Him in faith with all of my desires and daily struggles. He wants my heart. And He wants my heart to want Him.

God has always been the One who looks upon a person and sees the heart. I believe it is also significant that blood was spilled in Abel's sacrifice. We know the importance of a blood sacrifice for us to be made right with God. It's as old as the garden. Jesus is not only the Good Shepherd, but He lays down His life for the sheep.

There was another shepherd whom God called a "man after God's own heart." Probably the shepherd we all know the best—David.

READ 1 SAMUEL 16:1-13.

> Where was David when Samuel came to his house?

God noticed something about David's heart and chose him, a simple shepherd boy, to be the next king. This is one of my favorite stories in Scripture. It's such a great underdog story—the one who was least likely was God's choice. And I believe it's because God knew David's heart pursued His heart.

NOW TURN IN YOUR BIBLE AND READ EZEKIEL 34:1-23.

In the 2 columns below write down what the shepherds did that went against God's plan and then what the Lord said He would do as the true Shepherd. I'll give you an example to get us going.

What did the shepherds do wrong?	How would God handle the situation as the Good Shepherd?
They were feeding themselves instead of sheep.	God will rescue the sheep from their mouths.

God's plan is to have one Shepherd. And He is coming, according to Ezekiel.

Now, let's turn over to the New Testament and see the announcement of this prophecy fulfilled with the birth of Jesus.

READ LUKE 2:1-14.

Who were the first people to be told about the about the arrival of our Savior (v. 8)? *Country Shepherd*

Lastly, there is a reference to feeding sheep in John 21. You, like me, may have heard this passage many times, but I recently discovered something new about these verses. In verse 15, we find the resurrected Jesus talking with Peter who has returned to his original occupation of fishing:

> Jesus said to Simon Peter, "Simon son of John, do you love me more than these?"
>
> JOHN 21:15

Jesus is asking Peter this of course, but the question could be asked of us, too. We all have our own "these" things that we sometimes choose over Jesus.

For Peter, here, the "these" Jesus could have been referring to might have been the large number of fish he had just caught.

> What are some of "these" in your life?

> How have you chosen "these" over Jesus?

This question pierces my soul. I wonder sometimes if I want the answer to the cry of my heart more than I want God's plan. Because this desire has become one of my "these."

What if God's plan is to change us through this before He changes our circumstances in this?

Perhaps, though, my Good Shepherd is leading me and loving me by saying "no" or "not yet." I know, this is hard, but what if God's plan is to change us through this before He changes our circumstances in this?

> Has this been true in your life? How so?

Peter knew what it was like to be a fisherman. But Peter's destiny was not to be a fisherman the rest of his life. However, when things got complicated Peter ran back to what was comfortable.

Let's take a closer look at the conversation Jesus has with Peter after His initial question.

> When they had finished eating, Jesus said to Simon Peter,
> "Simon son of John, do you love me more than these?"
> "Yes, Lord," he said, "you know that I love you."
> Jesus said, "Feed my lambs."
> Again Jesus said, "Simon son of John, do you love me?"
> He answered, "Yes, Lord, you know that I love you."
> Jesus said, "Take care of my sheep."
> The third time he said to him, "Simon son of John, do you love me?"
> Peter was hurt because Jesus asked him the third time, "Do you love
> me?" He said, "Lord, you know all things; you know that I love you."
> Jesus said, "Feed my sheep."
>
> JOHN 21:15-17

Here's what I find so fascinating about the directives Jesus is giving Peter: This is the exact pattern of the shepherds I saw caring for sheep in Israel today. This is how they care for their flock.

"FEED MY LAMBS"—In the morning the shepherd gets up early in the sheepfold and feeds the little lambs first. He might feed them out of special food that he collected and tucked in his pocket—things that would be tender for their stomach. He would pick up the little lambs. He would hold them and check them to make sure they were okay. He would call them by name because he knew the lambs that intimately.

"TAKE CARE OF MY SHEEP"—After he feeds the lambs, the shepherd then carefully leads the sheep down to a place where they can be fed. He leads them and cares for them.

"FEED MY SHEEP"—The last step once he has fed the lambs, cared for the sheep, and led them to a good pasture was to feed the sheep.[4]

So why is it so important to note that Jesus is giving these directives to Peter?

I believe Jesus is trying to turn Peter from a fisherman into a shepherd. Peter has finished his season of being a fisherman of fish. Jesus is asking Peter to love Him more than the life Peter has known. Now He is calling Peter to be a shepherd for the people. There is a big difference between a fisherman and a shepherd.

If you look back in John 21:11 it says, "So Simon Peter climbed back into the boat and dragged the net ashore. It was full of large fish, 153."

I love this strange detail tucked in the holy words of God because fishermen would have known exactly how many fish they would have kept. Fishermen quickly judged and counted the fish they caught. They threw out the small fish because they'd have to pay more in taxes than the fish was actually worth. They would look at the fish and say, "This one's in, this one's out, this one's in, this one's out." A fisherman would never pick up the fish, love the fish, make sure the fish is okay, or name the fish.

Peter had to be changed from a quick-judging fisherman into a caring shepherd. A shepherd of God's people.

> Jesus is trying to change something in us, too. How might God be changing you from who you were to who He wants you to be?

> Who may God be calling you to shepherd? Pray that you would be willing to step into that role in his or her life.

We've spent all this time talking about shepherds. All the way back to the garden. We've seen examples of good shepherds and bad shepherds and a promise in Ezekiel that God was going to send one Shepherd to care for the entire flock. Then, Jesus was born and God couldn't wait to announce the news to, of course, shepherds. And in one of His last conversations on earth He directed Peter to shepherd His people. It's beautiful, isn't it?

Shepherds were the outcasts. The smelly ones. The ones who really couldn't even keep the law of the Sabbath because they couldn't take a day off from their duties. These are the ones the angels appeared to first. They appeared to shepherds to tell them that the Good Shepherd had been born in a stable. I'm so thankful God chooses the least likely people to do His work because I am certainly one of them. Bless His holy name.

THE GOOD SHEPHERD

I've had a lot of bad guides in my life:

My dad who left? Bad guide.

Friends who chased the next best thing? Bad guides.

Relationships purely for acceptance sake? Bad guides.

All of those things and people pointed me in a direction, but it wasn't always a direction I wanted to go.

Then one day a good guide came into my life. A girl I not-so-affectionately called my Bible friend. She honestly got on my nerves with all her Bible verse quoting. I wasn't on good terms with God at that point in my life. I didn't want to believe God even existed. And I certainly wasn't reading the Bible.

I made all of this very known to my Bible friend. But in her gentle, kind way she kept slipping me notes of truth with gently woven verses tucked within. And one day, one verse cracked the dam of my soul. Truth slipped in and split my hard-hearted views of life open just enough for God to make Himself known to me.

I held that simple note with one Bible verse scribbled on the front as the tears of honest need streamed down my cheeks. My stiff knees bent. And a whispered, "Yes, God," changed the course of my life.

My Bible friend had reached me. Now I will never doubt the power of one woman reaching into the life of another woman with some written whisper of love.

In biblical times, you might have said that my friend was good at shepherding—gently leading and guiding me toward life just as a shepherd would with his sheep.

In today's Scripture passage, Jesus refers to Himself three times as the Good Shepherd. In each of the instances, though, He focuses on a particular aspect of what the Good Shepherd means. I'm so thankful we have record of Jesus unpacking this statement so fully. In our study today we will look at each of the three aspects and see what God might want to say to us through them.

PLEASE READ THE ENTIRE PASSAGE FOR TODAY, JOHN 10:11-39, SO YOU HAVE A FEEL FOR THE WHOLE CONTEXT.

Before we jump into what the Good Shepherd does, it's important to know who the Good Shepherd is. The Greek word for *shepherd* in John 10:14 is *poimēn*. This specific word is used 18 times in the New Testament and John uses it the most frequently with 6 instances all within John 10. As we look elsewhere in the Scriptures we see that this is the same word used in Hebrews 13:20 that describes Christ as our "Great Shepherd."

For us to remember and consider Christ as our Great and Good Shepherd should be something that we both cherish and find comfort in. The early church intentionally remembered Jesus as Shepherd (Matt. 9:36; 26:31; 1 Pet. 2:25) and even applied Old Testament passages to Him that pictured God as Shepherd, such as Psalm 23:1.[5]

As we dig deeper into the Greek word for *good* in John 10:14, we find that it is not simply the opposite of bad. This specific word *kalos* also holds the connotation of noble, honorable, worthy. It points us to a sense of awe that suggests Christ is not just "good," but He is captivating and deserves praise. As we consider what the Good and Great Shepherd does, we can be encouraged in knowing that He is the perfect shepherd we as His sheep are drawn to follow.[6]

First, what does the Good Shepherd *do* (John 10:11)?

Jesus willingly laid down His life for us, His sheep. Jesus is the final atoning sacrifice for our sins. The old sacrificial system of bringing a sheep or other animal to the altar is complete now that Jesus chose to lay down His spotless, perfect life for us. The provision of a sacrifice to cover sin is *atonement*.

Take a second and let this truth sink in. If you've been a Christian a while you've heard this before, many times. After hearing it over and over again, our wonder of this revelation can become lost, numb, and just something else you hear. Don't let it be the case for you today. Let it simmer. Let it soak into the deepest, sacred parts of your heart.

Remember, the Jewish people of that time knew about the sacrificial system. There were many rules when it came to bringing sacrifices to God. The regulations set in motion by God Himself in Exodus and Leviticus had become a part of their normal rhythms and routines. All religious people knew them well.

For Jesus to come and say He was going to be laying His life down for His people so that the sacrificial system would no longer be needed would be astounding to witness. Imagine hearing that for the first time. After all, in the sacrificial system they knew it was the sheep being sacrificed, laying down its life for the shepherd. Here, Jesus turns it around and becomes the Lamb of God and takes on the sins of His sheep. Our Shepherd trades places with us.

Second, what does the Good Shepherd *know* (John 10:14)?

Not only does the Shepherd know the sheep, the sheep know Him. I wanted to understand more about that word *know* in this passage so I looked up its meaning. The Greek word that is used here is: *ginóskō*. The definition of the word according to the NAS Exhaustive Concordance is: "to come to know, recognize, perceive."[7] That doesn't seem helpful at first glance, but digging in a little deeper I found out something very interesting.

There are two major words in Greek that translate into our one word *know*. One of the words is *eido*, and it means "to know, remember, or appreciate."[8] This is more head knowledge, or facts. For example, I know who the president is. I know facts. I know my address. I know what my friends look like. Then there is *ginóskō*, which is used in the passage we're looking at. In this instance it means to know from experience. It implies more of a heart knowledge than a head knowledge. It's really knowing someone. This is the knowing a mother has with the cry of her child. Or best friends knowing how to finish each other's sentences. Or a spouse knowing how to make the other smile.

> To make this personal, write out something or someone you have head knowledge of *(eido)* and something or someone you have heart knowledge of *(ginōskō)* below:
> Head knowledge:

> Heart knowledge:

Jesus has both head knowledge and heart knowledge of you. He knows the number of hairs on your head. But He doesn't only know facts about you; He also knows your heart.

Let's turn that around, though, and look at it from the other side. Not only does He know us, He wants us to know Him in that same heart knowledge kind of way.

 What is a head knowledge fact that you know about God?
(Example: He created the universe.)

 What are some heart knowledge experiences that you know about God?
(Example: He cares for me so deeply that He has walked with me step by step through some of the hardest times of my life.)

> Third, and lastly, what does the Good Shepherd *give* (John 10:28)?

Not only does He give His sheep eternal life, there is no snatching the sheep out of His hand. Yes, we are going to mess up and stray away from God from time to time, but this promise still holds true.

Before we finish this week's lesson let's take a moment to revisit our discussion on the sheep gate. One of the interesting aspects of the sheep gate is that it was also a physical gate in the city of Jerusalem. If we look back to Nehemiah in the Old Testament, the people of Israel were just returning from exile and were in the process of rebuilding. The Sheep Gate (also known as the Lion's Gate and

The Sheep Gate in Jerusalem

Stephen's Gate) was built by Eliashib and his brothers (Neh. 3:1) and was built near the pool of Bethesda, also close to the temple. It was common for animals and sheep to enter through this particular gate for cleaning and cleansing before they went to the temple for sacrifice.[9]

In John 14:6, Jesus says, "I am the way and the truth and the life. No one comes to the Father except through me." Not only is Jesus the Good Shepherd who gives and lays down His life for His people, but He is also the Sheep Gate for the people of God to access and enter into the presence of God. Jesus gives us access to the Father so that we can live in intimacy and relationship with Him.

Perhaps you feel like you are wandering this world with no shepherd, no one to guide you or invest in you. Please know that Jesus Himself wants to be your Shepherd. And not just any shepherd—a GOOD Shepherd. A Shepherd who proved His love by laying down His life for His sheep, who wants to know you and be known, and wants to guide you through this life to eternity to live with and enjoy the presence of God.

OPTIONAL
READ JOHN 10–13.

Good questions to ask as you read are:
What does this passage teach me about God?

_____

_____

_____

_____

_____

_____

_____

_____

_____

_____

What does this passage teach me about myself?

_____

_____

_____

_____

_____

_____

_____

_____

_____

_____

What do I need to do as a result of reading this passage?

_____

_____

_____

_____

_____

_____

_____

_____

_____

_____

_____

_____

_____

_____

_____

_____

_____

_____

_____

_____

_____

_____

_____

As you read <u>John today</u>, see which of these attributes of God are exemplified and write out any thoughts you have about them.

Compassionate	Good	Faithful	Holy	Patient	Wise
Generous	Loving	Just	True	All-Knowing	
All-Powerful	Eternal	Gracious	Merciful	Faithful	

Video Session 4

WATCH VIDEO SESSION 4 AND RECORD YOUR NOTES BELOW.

Scripture in this video session:
Psalm 23 • John 10:7-11,14-16 • Psalm 139:14 • Jeremiah 50:6

Video sessions available for purchase
at www.lifeway.com/findingIAM

group guide

VIDEO GROUP DISCUSSION QUESTIONS

After watching the video, discuss the following questions in your group.

1. This particular video speaks of the gap between expectations and reality—how, often times, disappointment can grow there. How have you seen that happen in your life and how do you combat it?

2. How can you feel God's hand of restoration in your soul but maybe not see things change in your circumstances as you'd hoped? Discuss the difference if a personal example comes to mind.

3. What "deep ruts" have you created in your daily life of walking with God that you rely on? Or what "deep ruts" have you seen others before you form that you'd like to walk in?

4. How have you let the pursuit of temporary happiness sidetrack you from God's path for your life?

5. Why is it sometimes hard to be the sheep and let yourself be led by a shepherd? How can you let go of control this week and let Jesus guide you as your Good Shepherd?

6. In Psalm 23:2-3, the Lord/Shepherd does what four things? Which of those four things resonates with you most right now?

Life

I AM THE RESURRECTION AND THE LIFE.

JOHN 11:25

I AM THE WAY AND THE TRUTH AND THE LIFE.

JOHN 14:6

RESURRECTION LIFE

There's this little painting that hangs in my home. It makes me smile. Most people wouldn't consider it a masterpiece. I only paid $5 for it at an estate sale, but I like it because it speaks redemption to my soul every time I look at it.

I don't know what happened to the gal who painted it. All I know is it seems something about her life fell apart. And one day a company opened her front door to strangers. They walked through all the sacred spaces she once called home and bought the stuff her life had collected. I guess I'm too sentimental to attend estate sales. I couldn't stand it.

But I also couldn't leave without rescuing something in her creative collection. Based on the supplies for sale, I discerned she was a painter. I had the strangest notion to go on a wild adventure to find this unknown painter friend. I pictured it like an epic scene in a movie where the music crescendos and I find her living in a New York high rise. I would knock on her door and make the great assumption that she would be thrilled with my announcement.

"I just want you to know I love your work. It was not in vain. I bought one of your paintings and it speaks a message of redemption to me every day. And I treasure it."

Surely then she would get misty eyed, invite me in for coffee, and share the story how she lost it all in that hard season, but it opened the door for her to gain so much more.

She would tell me the devastatingly beautiful story of lies and loss. I would taste the bitter pill she could have swallowed. But then I would feel the grip of grace that rescued her from the pit. I would cry at the crescendo where God Himself becomes the great lover of her soul and the guide that got her here. We would hug. Exchange numbers. Become wonderful unlikely friends. She would go on to be a famous painter. And live happily ever after.

Roll credits.

But life isn't usually as epic and nicely neat as what we see on movie screens. It's untidy and unruly and so unpredictable that our fragile hearts get broken at best, crushed at worst. And sometimes it's just easier to run away than to risk letting the shards of the fallout cut away the little bit of life still left in us.

No crescendo to the music. No epic arc to the story. No lasting friendship. No credits to roll. Just a $5 painting that hangs in my kitchen. And that's all I know.

Life sometimes keeps us from details that are better left alone. It keeps some of the blanks blank on the outline of this message.

Does it ever drive you crazy when a speaker gives you an outline with blanks but then skips some of the points? Me too.

We like complete outlines. All the blanks filled in. All the gaps closed. All the details disclosed. And all the why questions answered to our satisfaction.

But that's not the way life is. Some speakers are disorganized and forgetful. Some gaps too wide to close. Some details are forgotten or simply edited out of the storyline. And there are some questions for which there are no apparent answers. I believe that's the way God wants it. Our all knowing God not only allows this but actually designed life to be this way.

Without blanks, we would have no room for Him to enter in and write His answers. For Him to become the way when there is no way. For Him to be the truth when lies long to be what consume our thoughts. For Him to be the life He's designed on the other side of our crumbling attempts to control our stories. Our God is not fickle, forgetful, or fragile in any way. He does not make mistakes. He purposes the gaps. He allows sacred spaces and blank places. He leaves room.

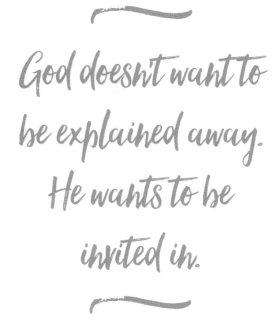

God doesn't want to be explained away. He wants to be invited in.

If we had all the blanks filled in we would explain away God's part in our story. God doesn't want to be explained away. He wants to be invited in. He wants us to make room for His additions to our story.

One time God was told "there is no room," and he turned an ordinary stable into an unforgettable sanctuary. "No room" became a space through which Jesus Christ stepped through glory to the grit and grime of this sin-soaked world. What did He come to bring? Redemption. And what do the blanks and unanswered questions of your life provide space for? Redemption.

So why can I never know the details of my kitchen painting? Redemption.

Which brings me to the reason why I want to make sure to have you read this, right now, today. If I were you, I would wonder why the details of my secret sorrow were left out. I might even be tempted to ponder, wonder, guess, and speculate. Fill in the gaps. Mull over the mystery.

What are the blanks in your life and the unanswered questions you long to have filled in?

As I go through this study with you, I'm a participant. I'm bringing my own painful realities to Jesus and asking Him to personalize these "I AM" statements so they leap from my Bible and into my soul.

Here I sit alongside you, eagerly inviting Jesus into my own unknowns. Gripping my Bible as the sweetest love note anyone has ever dared write to me. And I'm gazing at a $5 painting in my kitchen that radiates not just redemption but an absolute certain resurrection and life.

Today I want us to look at the seventh and final miracle of Jesus in the Gospel of John, and the fifth I AM statement. We will cover the whole chapter of John 11 today, but let's take it in two sections.

READ JOHN 11:1-27.

What is the I AM statement found in this passage?

Jesus told this powerful I AM statement to one woman—who was that woman?

Am I the only one who is fascinated that Jesus tells this monumental I AM statement to Martha? Not to the Jewish leaders, not to the disciples, not to Mary who sat at Jesus' feet, but to Martha. One woman. I'm so thankful that we have record of this statement, but I'm also thankful that Jesus is so intentional with this one woman. We don't know all the reasons why she may have needed to hear this word, but I'm certain that Jesus had a reason for telling it to her first.

Jesus is intentional with you too. He is the master of speaking to our hearts. He speaks to us in so many different ways. Sometimes loud. Sometimes soft. Sometimes He says hard things. Challenging and overwhelming things. Sometimes He says just what we need to hear to calm our souls. Sometimes He speaks to us in ways we may not understand in the moment but that we desperately need for the days to come.

Maybe all you needed to hear today is this one thing—God still speaks. To each of us. Individually. Right where we are.

This question might be one that you have to sit and ponder. Looking back over your last few days or weeks, what do you think God might be specifically saying to you right now? If you don't have a stirring in your heart of what God might be speaking to you personally, remember you can always hear Him speak through His Word. So consider these verses and what God might be saying to you:

 John 11:4

 John 11:25

John 11:26

Let's be sure our timeline here is correct. Lazarus became ill. His sisters Mary and Martha sent Jesus a message to tell Him. Jesus waited two extra days where He was and then headed to Bethany to where Lazarus was. In that day, tradition said the spirit of the person who died hovered over the body for three days and then departed.[1] John 11:17 tells us that by the time Jesus arrived Lazarus had been dead *four days*. All hope was lost. Lazarus was dead. You could say there were a lot of blanks left unfilled. But Jesus had a purpose.

When Jesus arrived in Bethany, Martha went to meet Him on the road.

You've been there, haven't you? When someone you love is diagnosed. When the timetable of someone's life is cut too short. It's gut wrenching. It's not fair. Jesus got word that His friend was sick, yet He waited. He seemingly did nothing.

Seemingly.

Take a moment and look at John 11:5-6 again. Does anything seem out of place to you?

The Scriptures say that Jesus loved Martha, her sister (Mary), and Lazarus. Here's where things get peculiar. Verse 6 says, "So when he heard that Lazarus was sick, he stayed where he was two more days."

Why do you think Jesus waited two extra days after hearing that Lazarus was ill before He traveled back to Bethany?

If I love someone and they get deathly sick, my initial reaction would not be to wait around a few more days! I would be frantically trying to find the next flight to get to them or jump in my car and drive there as fast as I could. Jesus' response on the surface seems peculiar, but some careful observations throughout the rest of this story give us insight into the possibility for why Jesus delayed His departure.

TAKE A MOMENT AND READ OVER JOHN 11:4-15 AGAIN, PAYING SPECIAL ATTENTION TO VERSES 4, 11, AND 15.

Jesus was very specific as to why He was going to see Lazarus. Verse 4 tells us that the purpose was for the glory of God to be displayed through this illness and so that the Son of God may be glorified.

What questions do you think Martha and Mary had unanswered at this moment? What would you have asked Jesus if you were in their positions?

As Jesus was drawing near, Martha runs out to meet Him and begins an incredibly faith-filled conversation.

> "Lord," Martha said to Jesus, "if you had been here, my brother would not have died."
>
> JOHN 11:21

Martha's faith was real. She believed Jesus could do miracles. She knew He could heal people. But this situation was hopeless, right? Lazarus was dead. As we read verses 21-22 we see Martha engaging in a conversation with Jesus that many of us find ourselves in. Imagine the agony and pain of knowing if Christ had been present, He could have saved her brother. In the midst of this reality Martha still confesses the might of Christ, acknowledging that Jesus can ask anything of the Father and it would be granted to Him. But Martha was missing the point.

She was looking forward to a future resurrection when Jesus wanted her to focus on what He was going to do in the present. She had given up hope of seeing Lazarus alive in the present.

What hopeless situation in your life have you given up on? What unanswered questions remain for you?

Even if our circumstances aren't good, His purpose always is.

Lord, give us relief from our unbelief.

We don't have to know all the details. We don't have to know the whys and the hows. But we can trust Jesus will accomplish His purpose. Even if our circumstances aren't good, His purpose always is. In verse 23, Jesus responded, saying that Lazarus would rise again!

How does this story remind you to not give up hope? Write a prayer to God and confess to Him that deep cry of your heart that has seemingly gone unanswered.

God may answer your prayer just the way you hoped. Or He may not. But at the end of the day will you trust His view of things? Will you trust that He knows the best way even if you don't? That's the question for all of us. Every day. Will you trust Him? Even if.

Divorce doesn't have the final say.

Cancer doesn't have the final say.

Infertility doesn't have the final say.

Rejection doesn't have the final say.

Heartbreak doesn't have the final say.

Doubt doesn't have the final say.

Even death doesn't have the final say.

We may be facing a delay, distraction, or even devastation for a season. But it is not a final destination. Resurrection is coming. For some of us, it will be like Lazarus and happen miraculously this day. But for all who trust in Jesus as Savior, whether our circumstances change or not, there is an eternal hope because His resurrection power has the final say.

Lazarus, Book of Hours, illuminated manuscript on Vellum. Bruges, 1465

In eternity, death doesn't win, Jesus does. ✝

What is the question Jesus asks Martha in verse 26? Write it below in big bold letters.

If This is as good as it Gets are you ok with it ??

READ VERSE 25 AGAIN.

Jesus begins with saying, "I AM" and ends with, "Do you believe this?"

That's the question for all of us, my friend. Will you believe Jesus at His word? Even if He delays His response? Even if you can't ever see the fruit in this life? Even if the blanks remain blank and the questions unanswered? Will you believe, even if …? Even if.

Oh Lord, give me relief from my unbelief too.

However it applies to your life, write your own version of this simple prayer here:

LET'S GO BACK TO LAZARUS. READ THE REST OF THE STORY IN JOHN 11:28-57.

We pick up in verse 28 with Martha calling her sister Mary to come see "the Teacher." It's interesting to see and compare the reaction and interaction between Jesus and these sisters. Notice, they both begin with a belief statement—if only Jesus was present their brother would be alive. From there, everything is different. Mary, taken over by grief and pure emotion, begins to weep. Compared to Martha who responds intellectually and reasons through her grief.

Lazarus's tomb in Bethany

As Mary and the crowd that followed her weep, Jesus "was deeply moved in his spirit and greatly troubled" (v. 33). Look closer at the Greek phrase used to describe Jesus' response. The word used is "*ἐμβριμάομαι*," *embrimaomai*, which refers to anger, outrage, and emotional indignation.[2]

Why do you think Jesus would have this strong feeling as He observes Mary and the crowd weeping?

He was angry, frustrated. Perhaps because those He loved, those whom He was closest to on earth, did not understand Him or His purpose. Despite all the miracles they'd seen, despite all the teaching they'd heard, they still did not understand He was the Resurrection and the Life.

Just a few verses later we come to the shortest verse in the Bible, which simply states, "Jesus wept." If we read this too quickly we can assume that Jesus wept for Lazarus whom He loved. But why would Jesus weep for someone He knew He was going to raise to life? Again, we see that Jesus' tears are motivated by the sight of destruction and despair in this world marked by sin and depravity.[3] Jesus cares about the condition of humanity and the effect that sin has on the people He loves.

Jesus' weeping isn't a sign that He doesn't have the power to right the wrongs. He does. And He did. God sent His Son to die on a cross to eternally wipe away the effects of sin. And in due time, there will be no more death, no more sin, no more weeping.

LET'S TURN TO VERSES 43-44.

By what means did Jesus raise Lazarus from the dead (see v. 43)?

Jesus' words bring life. When God speaks, things happen.

READ GENESIS 1:3 AND NOTE HOW GOD FORMED THE EARTH. BY HIS WORD.

How has God's Word brought you life lately?

God is the Creator of life. He made you. He is the Resurrection and the Life. He gave you life. And He gives you eternal life because of His sacrifice.

Eventually, Lazarus would die again. Though he was raised to life on earth, He wasn't yet resurrected. Death will happen to all of us. But death doesn't have the final say. Jesus has made a way for eternal life. His resurrection power will come to every believer in the dark hour of death, and every believer will be resurrected to eternal life. That is the glorious and great exclamation point to our grand love story with God.

THE LAST PASSOVER

The next I AM statement is found in John 14. To get there, though, we need to keep up with the story and examine John 12–13.

I'll summarize what happens in these two chapters and then we will spend some time looking at a few different parts of John 12 specifically.

If you are feeling ambitious today, go ahead and read chapters 12 and 13 to get the full story. If you don't have time, no worries—I've summarized it in the bullet points below.

JOHN 12:

- Six days before Passover, Jesus goes to Bethany for a dinner party in His honor.
- At that dinner party, Mary (the sister of Martha and Lazarus) anoints Jesus' feet with costly perfume.
- Judas feels like this is wasteful. Jesus rebukes Judas.
- Jesus rides into Jerusalem for the Passover celebration, on a donkey, with palm branches at His feet.
- Jesus predicts His own death.
- Jesus reminds the crowd that He is the Light of the world.

JOHN 13:

- Jesus' last supper with the disciples.
- Jesus washes the disciples' feet, including the feet of Judas. He commands His disciples to do the same type of service for others.
- Jesus tells His disciples that one of them will betray Him, and it turns out to be Judas. Judas leaves into the night.
- Jesus tells Peter that he will deny Jesus three times before the rooster crows.

The clock seems to speed up here. The critical hour is upon us. Can you feel the tension?

READ JOHN 12:9-19.

Why did the crowds flock to Jesus this time?

I feel like I am part of that crowd sometimes too. I come to see Jesus but I also want to experience the blessings of His hands. I come for both reasons. And I'm convicted. I come for Jesus plus something else.

What are some of your Jesus-plus items?

I wonder why we don't feel like Jesus is enough. Even from the garden we see this. Adam and Eve walked with God in the garden. They had all of their physical needs met. They had the relationship and love of God at their literal fingertips, and yet, their hearts were drawn to more. The crafty serpent interjects a thought that captivates Eve. The thought of "being like God" (Gen. 3:5). Ultimately, our desire to be like God stems from unbelief. We don't believe God is who He says He is. We don't believe He is sufficient, and because of our lack of trust, we wander and look to other things or our ability to provide what we don't think God will.

You are not alone if this is you. But by recognizing our lack of trust and bringing it to the light we can be reminded that in Jesus we truly have all we need and all we could ever want or desire.

You may be living under a promise of God but not yet see the fruit of that promise.

Write a prayer of confession to God and ask Him to help you long most of all for Jesus.

Let's read Old Testament prophecy about the king riding in on a donkey.

READ ZECHARIAH 9:9-10.

The Book of Zechariah was written after the Jewish people returned from their exile in Babylon. It was written in two parts. The first part (chapters 1–8) was written around October/November 520 B.C. (Zech. 1:1). The second part (chapters 9–14) doesn't give us an exact date, but the writing would have been around 475 B.C.[4]

Jesus was born between 4 and 6 B.C. and then this prophecy wasn't fulfilled until this moment when Jesus was 33 years old.

For me all this math stuff is hard, but try to calculate how many years it was between this prophecy in Zechariah and when Jesus fulfilled it.

The answer is 507-509 years. FIVE HUNDRED YEARS of an unfulfilled promise.

According to John 12:16, when did they realize what all this meant?

Zechariah never saw the fruit of the prophecy. And the disciples didn't see the meaning of what Jesus did here until much later. This information helps me when I start to struggle with the timing of circumstances in my own life. I often want to see the good God promises right now, but sometimes God's good answer is "not yet." There is a timing to everything. You may be living under a promise of God, but not yet see the fruit of that promise. You may be praying for something that has not happened yet and maybe even see no hope of it ever coming to pass. Though we may not understand, we must trust God's timing is perfect. ✈

God, even in those situations, is still very much at work. Even in the silence. Even in the unknown. Even when you can't see anything on the horizon.

> In what specific situation do you sense God might be at work even if you can't yet see the results?

When my grown daughters were teenagers I wanted them to want Jesus most of all in their hearts. But there was a season where I wondered if this would ever come to pass. A season where I cried myself to sleep most nights. A season full of worry and pain. And it certainly didn't help when I got an anonymous letter.

I opened the letter and my heart sank. It was from another mom who wanted to make sure I had a list of all the ways one of my daughters was falling short. There in black and white she listed my daughter's mistakes, shortcomings, and frailties. And then just to make sure I took her nameless letter seriously, she informed me she'd be sending a copy to my pastor.

My initial reaction was figure out who sent this so I could call her. Talk this through face-to-face. My aching heart wanted to assure her I was not only aware of some struggles my daughter was having but also working diligently to help her course correct. But as I reread the letter, I discerned it wasn't sent from a place of love for my family or a heart that wanted to help. From the language she used and the fact that there wasn't a way to contact her, it was obvious she didn't send it because she wanted the best for my daughter.

I sat on the edge of my bed and cried.

It's so hard to have someone attack you in an area that's already rubbed raw with hardship. Her letter was like a bullet straight to my heart. However, it was also a wake-up call to get more intentional in praying for my daughter. I thought about her struggles a lot. I talked about her struggles. I worried about her struggles.

But thinking about, talking about, and worrying about something is not the same as praying about it. I determined to turn this letter that felt like a bullet into a blessing by using it as a catalyst to ramp up my prayer life.

Through my tears I cried out to the Lord, "I will not sacrifice Your grace for my child on the altar of people's opinions. Of course I want my daughter to walk the straight and narrow path of great choices. But I trust You Lord to write her testimony. My main goal for her is not behavior modification but total heart transformation. I want her to want You, Lord, and Your best for her life. And God help me trust Your timing. I want things to be fixed with her right now. But, even more, I want You to fix things the best way. I realize that may take time. Give me the courage to not just pray about my daughter but to pray her all the way through this."

Praying her through the ups and downs wasn't easy. There were days I wondered if God was even hearing my prayers.

It's tough to pray someone all the way through a messy, hard, complicated situation and not see answers. Maybe you've been there. Maybe you are there now.

Is there a similar situation you're going through right now?

Can I speak hope into your heart with three ways to press through unanswered prayers?

1. KNOW WITH CONFIDENCE GOD HEARS YOUR PRAYERS.

> This is the confidence we have in approaching God: that if we ask anything according to his will, he hears us.
>
> 1 JOHN 5:14

Write out how this encourages you:

2. TRUST THAT PRAYER MAKES A DIFFERENCE, EVEN WHEN YOU DON'T SEE THE DIFFERENCE.

It may take a while for you to see God answer your prayers. But don't miss an "in the meantime answer" you can receive right away. This verse reminds us of the immediate answer to every prayer:

> Do not be anxious about anything, but in every situation, by prayer and petition, with thanksgiving, present your requests to God. And the peace of God, which transcends all understanding, will guard your hearts and your minds in Christ Jesus.
>
> PHILIPPIANS 4:6-7

When you pray, you can trust you are doing your part and God will certainly do His part.

What will guard your heart and mind in the process?

Write out how this encourages you:

 ## 3. TELL FEAR IT HAS NO PLACE IN THIS CONVERSATION.

These prayers are your gateway to feel an assurance you don't see yet. But fear will beg you to focus on the problem more than God's promises.

> So do not fear, for I am with you; do not be dismayed, for I am your God. I will strengthen you and help you; I will uphold you with my righteous right hand.
>
> ISAIAH 41:10

Write out how this verse encourages you:

God is still at work. Even in the unknown.

It's been several years since I got that hard letter that prompted more frequent prayers for my daughter. Only a few months into her freshman year at college, I went to go visit her and could hardly believe my eyes. She was a completely different girl.

At one point during our time together, I asked her, "What finally made following Jesus wholeheartedly click for you?" She said, "Mom, I've made friends who love Jesus. I saw a joy in them that I wanted. So, I started doing what they do even when I didn't want to. At first I thought getting up to do devotions was unrealistic, prayer meetings were boring, and listening to praise music excessive. But as I kept doing these things, the Lord started changing my thought patterns. And when I started thinking about life from the standpoint of truth, I had so much more joy."

She then paused and said words I've longed to hear and prayed to hear for so long, "Mom, I've just completely fallen in love with Jesus." I can hardly type those words without crying.

Here's my plea to you in this situation: Trust Him. When you are tempted to give up or stop trusting—don't. He is still at work even if we can't see it at this moment in time.

LAST THING FOR TODAY—READ JOHN 12:37-41.

These verses are both convicting and troubling to me. But can I offer a piece of encouragement? There are some passages of God's Word meant to convict and trouble us. This is a function of Scripture. These people who had been following Jesus and saw Him perform miracle after miracle still didn't believe Him. They could not accept His words even though they had seen His miraculous hand.

So, with that in mind, here is my final plea for the day. Don't forget what Jesus has done in your life thus far. Take a moment to remember some of the works of His hands and thank Him for it. I promise, tracing the hand of God in your life like this is good for your soul.

WAY, TRUTH, & LIFE

Today we are going to study Jesus' sixth I AM statement. Can you believe we are this far into the study? I hope you can sense me cheering you on as you dive into God's Word. Don't give up! I can't wait to see what God will continue to show us as we wrap up this study together.

Jesus' final two I AM statements are only said to His disciples.

KEEPING THAT IN MIND, READ JOHN 14:1-4.

What is the very first thing Jesus says to His disciples in 14:1?

Why is Jesus comforting His disciples at this time? To answer that, we have to take a look back at chapter 13. There are three big reasons why the disciples might be troubled.

Read the verses below and note each reason you think they might be troubled or in need of comfort during this time.
Reason 1: John 13:21-26

Reason 2: John 13:31-37

Reason 3: John 13:38

I'd be troubled too, wouldn't you? You can feel the tension rising, the heat turning up as we come to the part of the story we know so well.

It's within this context that Jesus tells His disciples to not allow their "hearts" to be troubled. The Greek word for *heart* is καρδία, (*kardia*), but it is not necessarily referring to our physical organ or even an emotional state of being. During the time of Jesus the "heart" was referenced as the center of human will.[5] So Jesus is really encouraging His disciples to be unwavering in their determination.

Do you realize that Jesus is about to walk into the hardest part of His earthly existence? He was about to be beaten and crucified for our sins on the cross and yet He is here comforting His disciples. He had every right to focus on Himself and prepare Himself for what was ahead, yet He chose to continue to provide teaching and comfort to those closest to Him. What a caring Savior. He truly is the God of all comfort.

As I read John 14:1-4 I am filled with questions. Where exactly is Jesus going? Where is this house? How do we get to the house? What will the rooms look like? What will we do in the house? I have the sense that the disciples also had some questions and thankfully Thomas is the one who voices a specific question.

READ JOHN 14:5-14.

I don't know about you but I'm so thankful Thomas didn't sit back and act like he knew exactly what Jesus was saying but decided to step up and ask Jesus to clarify. I know he gets a bad rap sometimes, but I can relate to him. I have many questions and when I can't see something clearly, I am going to go to Jesus for some clarification. Jesus said this I AM statement as a result of Thomas's question. I don't want to dive too far into this, but I think it deserves a mention. Jesus wants us to come to Him with our questions and concerns. If we do that, we may just get some of the sweetest, most important answers from the Savior.

What is the I AM statement Jesus makes in this section?

The Way, the Truth, and the Life. This I AM statement is the clearest example in Scripture of the certainty of Jesus being the only way to eternal life.

What makes you uncomfortable about this statement?

On the flip side, what is comforting about this I AM statement?

Jesus can handle any questions or hesitations you may have about this statement. Bring those concerns to Him. Let's take this statement a word at a time.

WAY (*HODOS* IN GREEK): a way, road, journey. [6]

This Greek word is not used very much in the New Testament, but Matthew 7:13-14 is one instance where we find it.
READ THOSE VERSES.

Write what you find out about the way (your translation may have the word *road* instead of *way*).

PROVERBS 14:12 IS ALSO TRANSLATED "WAY." READ IT AND SUMMARIZE IT IN YOUR OWN WORDS BELOW.

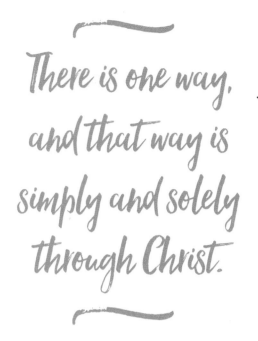

There is one way, and that way is simply and solely through Christ.

Some people in this world think they have the way figured out. But unless the way is Jesus, they are deceived. Jesus is stating very clearly that He is the Way. There is an exclusivity to this phrase, similar to John 10:7-9 where Jesus refers to Himself as the Sheep Gate. Jesus doesn't come to show a "better" way. There is no other way. There is one way, and that way is simply and solely through Christ.

TRUTH (*AL⊠THEIA* IN GREEK): truth, but not merely truth as spoken; truth of idea, reality, sincerity, straightforwardness.[7]

What part of that definition stands out to you the most today and why?

For me, it is straightforwardness. Sometimes I feel like Jesus is holding out on me. That He purposely is keeping something just out of my reach. This word, though, reminds me that He longs to tell me the truth. He longs to show me the way. It is not hidden, even though I may not see it clearly today.

WE SEE THIS GREEK WORD IN JOHN 8:32, TOO. TAKE A MOMENT AND READ THAT VERSE.

Do you equate truth with freedom? Why or why not?

As a society we can sometimes think truth and freedom are opposites. That freedom is all about whatever you might believe. That truth is restricting. But in this verse, we learn the opposite. Only in the truth can we be free.

Let's look again at Adam and Eve and how the enemy tried to twist God's truth to seem restrictive rather than protective.

READ GENESIS 2:15-16.

What are the first words God uses in His command to Adam?

NOW READ GENESIS 3:1 AND NOTICE HOW THE ENEMY TWISTS GOD'S COMMAND.

Write out what the serpent said to Eve.

God's words were full of freedom, "you are free," with one protective command to not eat from the tree of the knowledge of good and evil. But the enemy wanted Eve's focus to be on the one thing she couldn't have. And the enemy wants our focus to be there as well. Satan wants us to feel God is restrictive, unrealistic, and secretly holding out on us.

I have three dogs. But my two outside dogs, Champ and Chelsea, are sometimes delinquent. I love them. They love me. But they love running away more. Even though we don't have a fence, we have other systems in place to keep them safely at home.

I can't tell you the number of sleepless nights I've had fretting over my dogs. Several times we've enlisted our friends to pray for Champ and Chelsea. This sort of backfired on us once.

One of our friends knew Champ had gone missing and miraculously found him in a yard miles from our home. He was amazed Champ had run so far. He pulled into the driveway, coaxed Champ into his car, and called me with breathless excitement to announce he'd found my beloved dog.

But five minutes before my friend got to my house, Champ came home. When my friend pulled into my driveway carrying a Champ lookalike, we both about fell over. My friend had kidnapped someone else's dog—right from their front yard!

Oh my. It was time to do something.

I used to think invisible fences were cruel. I couldn't stand the thought of my dog getting a shock. So, I looked into getting a regular fence. But we live in the country and installing a regular fence was simply out of the question. An invisible fence it would have to be. After all, a shock to keep them inside the safe boundary is a lot better than what might happen outside the boundary.

God's truth is meant to be protective, not restrictive.

Boundaries aren't cruel barriers meant to keep my dogs from freedom. They are protective restrictions meant to define where safe freedom can be found.

My dogs aren't the only ones who need to remember this lesson. I need to remember this and apply it to the protective restrictions God has for me.

LIFE (Z⬜⬜ IN GREEK): life, both of physical (present) and of spiritual (particularly future) existence.[8]

You remember this word; we studied it back in Week 1. John uses this word 36 times in his Gospel. He truly believes that you can only find life, real life, meaningful life, through Jesus Christ.

READ DEUTERONOMY 30:19-20.

Note the three things that mean life according to verse 20.

Which of these three resonates with you most right now?

Spend some time now writing out a short prayer. Thank Jesus today that He is the Way, the Truth, and the Life and can give us this certainty. What a wonderful Savior.

DAY 4

PROPHECY FULFILLED

Jesus, through His I AM statements, makes a clear case for His identity. He is the Bread of life; He is the Light of the world; and He is the Way, the Truth, and the Life. Jesus can make these bold claims, these I AM statements, because they are true. The predictions about the Messiah in the Old Testament are fulfilled and proven true through Jesus.

Of all the I AM statements we've looked at, the Resurrection and the Life points most directly to our future hope for eternal life. Because Jesus tells us He is the only way, it is so important for us to see how His life is the fulfillment of prophecy.

Today we are going to take a look at many of those prophecies and see how Jesus fulfilled them. It is my hope that these truths boost your faith and trust in Him and help you rely on God's Word even more.

I love a chart. I am hoping you do too. Today's lesson will seem shorter in page length, but it is because I want you to spend time looking up the Scriptures and filling in the chart on the next page.

I've listed the general topic and the Old Testament and New Testament passage I want you to look up in column 1, column 2, and column 3. Your job is to look up the passage and fill in the prophecy fulfilled in column 4. I've filled in the first line for you to show you what I mean.

GENERAL TOPIC	OT PASSAGE	NT PASSAGE	PROPHECY FULFILLED
Christ's Birthplace	Micah 5:2	Matthew 2:1	*Born in Bethlehem*
Christ's Birth	Isaiah 7:14	Matthew 1:20-25	
Christ's Lineage	Genesis 49:10	Hebrews 7:14	
Jesus' Journey	Hosea 11:1	Matthew 2:14-15	
Jesus' Forerunner	Isaiah 40:3-4	Mark 1:2-8	
Christ's Words	Psalm 78:2-4	Matthew 13:10-13	
Jesus' Companions	Psalm 41:9	John 13:21-27	
Jesus' Trial	Isaiah 53:7	Mark 15:4-5	
Jesus' Crucifixion	Exodus 12:46	John 19:33-36	
Jesus' Sacrifice	Isaiah 53:5-12	Romans 5:6-8	

Gregg Matte, I AM Changes Who I AM (Ventura, CA: Regal, 2012), 178.

In addition to these 10, there are numerous passages that refer to the coming King and His kingdom (Isa. 62:11; Jer. 30:9; Dan. 2:44-45; 7:27; Mic. 4:1-8; Zech. 9:9-10). Consider that the Israelites who are now under the authority and rule of Roman occupation were desperate to be released and set free again. They were in eager anticipation for the return of this great and glorious King whom they thought would provide political and physical freedom. Earlier we briefly looked at Jesus' triumphal entry in John 12:12-15. Let's take a closer look at the expectations of the people compared to the purpose of Christ.

As we look at all these prophecies of the coming King and His kingdom, it's clear the Israelites have an expectation for Jesus to become their king on earth and right the political injustices they were facing. If that were true, the Messiah probably would have ridden in on a horse or stallion. However, when Jesus enters, He enters on a donkey! The significance of this is immense.

Not only was Jesus riding on a donkey the fulfillment of the prophecy of Zechariah 9:9, but it also signaled Jesus had a different plan and purpose. He didn't come to bring a temporary victory by becoming an earthly king through battle. He came to bring an everlasting victory by becoming the eternal King who died on a cross to save His people.

Throughout these prophecies we see that Jesus is in fact who He said He was and what was declared thousands of years earlier in the Scriptures. There is an important lesson to be learned about assumptions and expectations. In the account of the triumphal entry we are reminded that God's ways are sometimes opposite of what we want and expect. We need to remember to consider what God's purposes are and align our expectations and desires around His.

I hope that through these examples you can see that Jesus can indeed claim to be the Way, the Truth, and the Life because He is the Messiah that so many in the Old Testament prophesied about.

In the end, do you know what else this exercise does for my soul? It reminds me that God is a God of completion. He makes promises and then He fulfills them. Even if we don't see it in this life—He will complete what He has set out to complete.

OPTIONAL
READ JOHN 14–17.

Good questions to ask as you read are:
What does this passage teach me about God?

_____

_____

_____

_____

_____

_____

_____

_____

_____

_____

_____

What does this passage teach me about myself?

_____

_____

_____

_____

_____

_____

_____

_____

_____

_____

What do I need to do as a result of reading this passage?

_____

_____

_____

_____

_____

_____

_____

_____

_____

_____

As you read John today, see which of these attributes of God are exemplified
and write out any thoughts you have about them.

Compassionate	Good	Faithful	Holy	Patient	Wise
Generous	Loving	Just	True	All-Knowing	
All-Powerful	Eternal	Gracious	Merciful	Faithful	

_____

_____

_____

_____

_____

_____

_____

_____

_____

_____

_____

Video Session 5

WATCH VIDEO SESSION 5 AND RECORD YOUR NOTES BELOW.

Scripture in this video session:
Luke 10:38-42 • John 11 • Isaiah 29:13 • John 14:1-6 • Zechariah 14:4,6-9

Video sessions available for purchase
at www.lifeway.com/findingIAM

VIDEO GROUP DISCUSSION QUESTIONS

After watching the video, discuss the following questions in your group.

1. Martha and Thomas. You may have learned something new about them today. How do their stories resonate with you now?

2. What are some things that you think may be holding you back from experiencing the full resurrection power of Jesus?

3. Could you relate with the story about keeping parts of your life hidden because no good could come from sharing them? If so, and you feel comfortable, share with the group.

4. What label have you put on yourself that you sense Jesus wants you to take off today, so that He can resurrect your true identity?

Vine

WEEK 5

I AM THE TRUE VINE.

JOHN 15:1

#FINDINGIAM

DAY 1

I'M NOT GOOD ENOUGH

The party sounded amazing. The people I'd heard were going are easy to be with, incredibly fun, and all have mad skills in the kitchen. And when I saw the invitation posted on a friend's refrigerator I smiled at the creative brilliance.

The only problem was I didn't get one.

I'd been checking my mailbox for days. Every time I walked back down the driveway empty handed, I kept assuring my sinking heart that because we live in a more rural area my mail is always a day or two or even seven days behind everyone else's. No big deal.

But three days before the party when the invite still hadn't arrived I ran out of assurance. I lost the pep in my rally. And I realized I was, in fact, not on the guest list.

When I ran into one of the hostesses later that day I lobbed out the equivalent of a Hail Mary throw in the final seconds of a game, "What do y'all have going on this weekend?" And then I felt as pitiful as the quarterback who watches the opposing team take what would have been his shining star moment and turn it into an interception.

She replied, "We've got plans with friends most of the weekend but would love to catch up on Sunday after church."

That's when the hardest of all the realizations hit me. I wasn't invited because they simply hadn't thought to invite me. I wasn't in the circle of "weekend plans with friends." Immediately the thought that hopped on me and stuck with super glue tenacity was, "I'm not good enough."

I smiled and told her I'd check to see if that might work. I mean, checking my calendar was crucial because I was pretty slammed with plans that weekend as well. Indeed, my schedule was jam-packed full of all kinds of urgent plans with Netflix. And, hey, for an extra thrill I could always get a little jump on paperwork for tax returns not due for four more months.

I didn't want to feel pathetic but I did. Middle school had come for an unwelcome visit bringing with it all the wonky feelings wrapped up in: "I'm not good enough." I seriously thought by my 46th year of life these feelings would be but a vague memory in my way distant past. Like running while wearing a bathing suit. Or eating pizza at midnight. Or wearing your bangs teased so high people wonder if there's a nest in the front of your head. You reach a certain age where you realize that's no longer a good option for your life. So why is it still an option for a grown woman like me to feel like the lonely middle school girl that never got asked to this weekend's dance?

Since I had all kinds of thinking time during that weekend, I kept pondering that statement sitting on my heart, "You're not good enough." And finally in the late hours of Saturday night I had a slight breakthrough. "Good enough" is a terrible statement. Nobody ever wants their friends to say, "Well, I mean, you're good enough." I would never want my boss or my family to just say, "You are good enough." No child would ever want his or her parent to say, "You're good enough."

Absolutely not.

God made us to be amazing people who learn and explore and create and give. and delight and love. He made us full of potential and purpose. He made us to produce fruit. Good fruit. Fruit that brings glory to God, our vinedresser.

He made us to reach out, not pull back.

He made us to believe the best before assuming the worst.

He made us to freely give grace, realizing we so desperately need it ourselves.

He made us to add goodness, see the beautiful, and rest in the assurance of His lavish love for us.

Never ever for one second did God look at us and say, "My goal for this one is to simply be good enough."

Without Jesus we are selfish, self-focused, and all about our fruit bringing glory to ourselves. We work and strive and exhaust ourselves all for a pursuit that leaves us with a hallowed out feeling that there's got to be more to life than chasing what we want, hoping to feel good enough.

With Jesus, we are better than good enough because He steps in and fulfills what we cannot do on our own.

> JOHN 15:1 SAYS,
>
> "I am the true vine, and my Father is the gardener."

In essence, what Jesus is saying in this I AM passage is—I am doing what you could not do. I am the true Vine. Israel, you were supposed to be the vine, but you couldn't do it. So, I AM is coming and saying that He is about to step in and fulfill what you could not do.

We cannot do what God has called us to do without Him.

We are in that same boat, my friend. We cannot do what God has called us to do without Him. We are unable to be faithful to His commands. We have failed over and over just like the Israelites failed time and time again. The Jewish people hearing Jesus that day needed Him to step in as the true Vine. And we need Him to do that for us as well.

Do you feel that in your life? That sense that you are not enough? It sits deep in our souls most days. Buried down deep where we try to keep it hidden. We want so much to be enough. To be what God wants us to be. I know we try so hard. But the cloud still looms and tells us we are simply not enough.

Today, I want you to do something that might seem counterintuitive at first—embrace that truth instead of trying to cover it up. Step in it for a minute with me; you are not alone.

> In what ways do you feel "not enough" today or this week?

> How have you tried to cover this up in your life by doing something? What is it you do to try to cover it up?

> Did it work? Did it mask the feeling? If so, for how long?

Have you ever secretly wondered if the reason your longing has gone unmet is because you aren't good enough? I have. And it took me years to bring that before the Lord and let Him tenderly speak that truth over me.

> Write out a prayer to the Lord asking Him to speak to you tenderly and personally about this today. Here are some verses you can incorporate into your prayer: Ephesians 2:10; Romans 8:38-39; James 1:2-4; 1 Peter 2:9; and Zephaniah 3:17.

Might this longing be the very thing that helps you stay most deeply connected to the Vine and therefore be the catalyst to you producing rich fruit in your life? And then imagine the people that would so deeply be blessed by your fruit. Write about that here.

Here's what I want to take your hand and whisper to you today. Free yourself from trying to be the true vine. You are not it. That's what Jesus does for us.

We run at a breakneck pace to try and achieve what God simply wants us to slow down enough to receive. We receive from Him everything we need to produce the fruit, therefore we must remember to stay connected to Him.

> I am the vine; you are the branches. If you remain in me and I in you, you will bear much fruit; apart from me you can do nothing.
>
> JOHN 15:5

Notice how Jesus requests that we remain. Jesus doesn't participate in the rat race. He's into the slower rhythms of life, like abiding, delighting, and dwelling—all words that require us to trust Him with our place and our pace.

 Let Him be the true Vine today. Rest in and thank Him for being the true Vine that we desperately need.

PRUNING, ABIDING, AND BEARING FRUIT

Now that we've learned that we are not the true vine, and that Jesus is, we can turn our attention to our role in the vineyard.

THE I AM PASSAGE FOR TODAY IS FOUND IN JOHN 15:1-11.

Read it and answer the questions below. I know these questions are simple, but they give us a foundation for our time together today.

Who is the true Vine? *Jesus*

Who is the Gardener?

Who are the branches? *We are*

We are the branches. This is only the second time in an I AM statement that Jesus tells us specifically what we are. The first one was when Jesus said that He was the Light of the world—He also told us, shockingly, that we are also the light of the world (Matt. 5:14). Here we learn we are not the vine, but rather the branches connected to it.

There are three key parts of this passage: pruning, abiding, bearing fruit.

PRUNING

We might as well get the yucky stuff out of the way first, right? Pruning is not really a topic we study all the time, because, well—it's not fun to talk about. We don't think we want to be pruned. It implies pain. It implies that something will be taken away from us. It reminds us that we can't have it all.

> He cuts off every branch in me that bears no fruit, while every branch that does bear fruit he prunes so that it will be even more fruitful.
>
> JOHN 15:2

Let's dissect this verse a bit. Fill in the blanks below about what happens in each situation.

If the branch does bear fruit, ~~cut off~~ *Prunes so be even more fruitful* ~~leave it alone~~

If the branch does not bear fruit, *cuts off* .

If a branch on a tree or vine does not bear fruit, it gets cut off entirely. Gone. No more. No fruit on it, it is cut off. That makes sense to me.

If a branch does bear fruit—it gets pruned. Wait a second, what? The branch is bearing fruit! So, why on earth does it get pruned?

No fruit on the branch—it's gone. Fruit on the branch—it gets pruned. Does this feel like a no-win situation here, or is it just me?

Where is the verse that says, "Way to go, branch that bears fruit! I will leave you alone because clearly you are doing something right. Keep up the good work! Carry on with all the wonderful things you are doing right!"?

Why do you think Jesus says that even if branches are bearing fruit they must be pruned? *be more fruitful*

How does God cut off or prune in our lives today? What are the results of His pruning? *more fruitful*

Here's some good news for you. God isn't pulling off dead branches or pruning the fruit because He doesn't want you producing fruit. He is doing it because He wants you to be even more fruitful. He wants you to bear even more fruit!

ABIDING

> Abide in me, and I in you. As the branch cannot bear fruit by itself, unless it abides in the vine, neither can you, unless you abide in me.
>
> JOHN 15:4, ESV

Some of your translations will use *remain* here instead of *abide*—whatever word your version of the Bible may say, this word comes from the Greek root word *menó* which means: to stay, abide, remain, wait.[1]

I don't know about you, but I am not the best at this particular verb. I far prefer terms like go, move, be productive, keep the wheels turning. I mean, there is so much to do every day, right? To wait, remain, stay, and abide seem like the opposite of productivity.

I'm asked lots of questions when I meet people at conferences. Practical questions, like, "How did you get started speaking and writing?" Heart-wrenching questions—"How did you forgive those that hurt you so much?" Hard questions, such as, "Why would God let this happen?" And honest questions, like, "How can I find God, connect with God, in the midst of my everyday life?"

It's that last question that compels me to do what I do every day. It's what brings me to sit at the computer and tangle with words and truths and vulnerable admissions. It's what compels me to split my heart wide open and let people see the not so great stuff about me mixed with the gracious goodness of God.

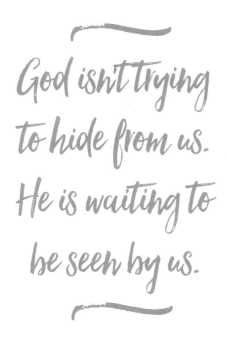

God isn't trying to hide from us. He is waiting to be seen by us.

Because if I can help a soul find an authentic, honest way to connect with God, all the other questions will settle down a bit. Wait more patiently. Maybe decide it's okay if they go unanswered.

Connection with God is such a deeply personal and uniquely individual process. Surely it can't be reduced to a few points and a poem. But there are three words that stir me. Move me. Show me. Propel me. Three words I hear Jesus saying over and over: "Abide in Me."

Tucked within these three words, four syllables, nine letters is the wild secret of deep connection with God. If we want to know God, we have to abide in Him.

How do we abide in Him?

Follow His instructions, His heart, and His example.

Not just follow along as we mindlessly repeat the words of the Jesus songs and scribble some notes during the pastor's sermon. No. Really follow. Follow hard. Follow passionately. Follow fully. Follow with engaged minds and willing hearts and open hands and ready feet.

And where can we start this kind of following?

By asking God to let us see Him.

When we pray, we invite the divine presence of the Almighty God to do life with us that day. Watch for Him. Look for Him. Make the connection of things that happen as direct evidence of His hand at work. In us. Around us. In spite of us. Ask Him to help you see His activity as you seek to follow more fully. And He will. Rest assured God isn't trying to hide from us. He is waiting to be seen by us.

What does remaining/abiding in Christ look like in our daily lives?

I love this quote from author and pastor Warren Wiersbe:

"To put it another way, the better we know Jesus, the more we will love Him. The more we love Him, the more we will obey Him, and the more we obey Him, the more we will abide in Him. The more we abide in Him, the more fruit we will bear; and the more fruit we bear, the more we will experience life overflowing. It's somewhat of a spiritual chain reaction, and it begins with our decision to spend quality time with our Lord each day."[2]

BEARING FRUIT

> I am the vine; you are the branches. If you remain in me and I in you, you will bear much fruit; apart from me you can do nothing.
>
> JOHN 15:5.

We bear fruit by staying connected to the vine. Pure and simple. There is no other way to bear fruit.

The good news here, though, is this is our one job to do—stay connected. Are you worried you aren't bearing enough fruit in your life? Stay connected to Jesus. It's that simple. And it's that hard.

I'm so prone to disconnecting and then trying to muster up some fruit on my own. But the fruit I bear isn't lasting fruit—unless I'm connected to the vine. Continually relying on Him and going back to the source is the key to a fruitful life. See what I mean about easy and hard?

Here's the kicker, though—take a second look at John 15:8. It is to God's glory that we what?

Does that surprise anyone besides me? God wants us to bear much fruit. He wants our life to be profoundly fruitful. In fact, that is why He prunes us—so we can be *more* fruitful.

You may feel like God is pruning you right now. Perhaps it isn't because He wants you to stop doing what you are doing; perhaps He wants you to be even more fruitful in that area. Sometimes He removes branches that aren't bearing fruit, and other times He prunes where you are fruitful so that even more fruit will come.

How does this speak to your life right now? What areas do you feel like God is pruning or removing in you so you can bear more fruit?

In all of this, remember, bearing fruit takes time. Fruit doesn't just pop up overnight. Fruit comes in seasons. Just because we don't see tangible fruit in an area of our lives right now doesn't mean that God isn't working. Our job is to abide. Remain. Let's keep doing that and watch to see how God might work in our lives.

And just like that, Jesus is done telling us His I AM statements. You've studied all seven. Look how far we've come! But, we aren't done yet. Jesus still has a few more things to say to us.

7 I AM

DAY 3

FINAL WORDS

The second half of John 15 is important for us to consider as it features some of Jesus' final words on earth to us. Those final words can be so precious and so dear. We can be sure that Jesus didn't say these words lightly. Let's read them together.

READ JOHN 15:12-27.

> Are these the type of final words you might expect to hear from Jesus? Why or why not?

As you are aware, much of this study has been centered around the deep desires of your heart. I hope that by studying these I AM statements you have felt God speak to you about those heart desires with His words and His love.

One reason you may feel a sense of lack in your life is because you feel you have a love deficit. Life can get that way sometimes. You get so busy going and going and doing and doing and start to feel that grind of keeping up and checking off every item on your to-do list. In doing this, you may forget that you are deeply and wholeheartedly loved.

When we feel like we aren't adequately loved we can be tempted to turn to the wrong things. Let God remind you today that you are deeply loved by Him. Right where you are.

When we know we are fully loved by God, we are then freed up to truly love one another well. We love better when we realize we are loved fully by our Creator. And that is Jesus' command in these verses—love one another as Jesus has loved us. In doing so, we will bear much fruit.

Who in your life may need a little extra love from you? How can you show them love today or in the week to come?

How have you found that loving others helps you? Think of an example when you focused on others instead of yourself and note how your attitude changed for the better.

Lately I've felt challenged to look at love a little differently. Sometimes in the gut honest quietness of my heart, I look at love through the eyes of what it will offer me. I hold out the little cup of my heart to people I love, "Will you fill my empty spaces? Today will you do that one really thoughtful thing and make me feel like I'm the most noticed and special woman in the world?" Then I hold it out to my children, "Will you fill up my empty spaces? Will you do something today that makes me look really good as a mom so I'll feel a little more validated?" Then I hold it out to my ministry, "Will you fill up my empty spaces? Will you provide something today that makes me feel more significant?"

If my only view of love is what it will give me, love from others will fail me every time. It's not that love fails. It's that other people were never meant to be my god. God's love never fails. This is what God is describing in 1 Corinthians 13:8.

> Love never fails. But where there are prophecies, they will cease; where there are tongues, they will be stilled; where there is knowledge, it will pass away.
>
> 1 CORINTHIANS 13:8

Even a wonderful family and thriving ministry can never truly fill me up, right all my wrongs, and meet my deepest needs.

No, I can't read 1 Corinthians 13 with eyes hungry to see what love should give me and then demand it from those around me. I should read those steadfast Scriptures with the realization that this is the kind of love I can choose to give.

I can choose that my love will be patient. My love will be kind. My love won't keep a record of wrongs—ouch, that's a hard one. I can choose that my love will protect and persevere. And I can choose to lay the cup of my heart at Jesus' feet and stop twirling, twirling, twirling, hoping—no, demanding—that those around me do things for me they were never meant to do.

Love isn't what I have the opportunity to get from this world. Love is what I have the opportunity to give. Loving others is one of the keys to feeling love. But loving others can be ridiculously hard.

Thankfully, Jesus doesn't expect us to love the world in our own strength. He sends the Advocate (v. 26). I love that the Holy Spirit is called the Advocate. Other words used here are Helper and Counselor. I love those too. It reminds me that we are not alone; we have someone wise and loving backing us up.

Love isn't what I have the opportunity to get from this world. Love is what I have the opportunity to give.

The Greek word for *Advocate is paraklétos*. It means: called to one's aid or (a) an advocate, intercessor, (b) a consoler, comforter, helper, (c) Paraclete.[3]

This specific Greek word is only used a handful of times in the Bible and each time by John. Let's look up each reference to this Advocate, Helper, Counselor and see what we can learn.

Match the verses below to what we learn about the Advocate.

___ 1. John 14:16-17   a. Jesus will send the Helper when He goes away.

___ 2. John 14:26   b. He will be with you forever; also called Spirit of Truth.

___ 3. John 16:7   c. He speaks to the Father on our behalf when we sin.

___ 4. 1 John 2:1   d. He will teach you everything and remind you of Jesus' words.

Which of these speak to you today and why?

Romans 8:26 is one of my favorite verses that refers to how the Holy Spirit helps me with my weak places. We all have them. Places inside that make us wonder if we'll ever get it together like those "together people." Places that make us feel less than. Less than victorious. Less than a conqueror. Less than strong. My weak places frustrate me. And yet I refuse to resign that I can't ever change.

With the power of Christ all things can be made new. All broken things are subject to restoration.

Let this verse breathe a little life into your weakness today. Whatever it is, however large it may loom:

> The Spirit helps us in our weakness. We do not know what we ought to pray for, but the Spirit himself intercedes for us through wordless groans.
>
> ROMANS 8:26

We don't have to have all the answers. We don't have to make suggestions to God. It's okay to be so tired of our weak places that we run out of words to pray.

Look at the beautiful verses written to us Jesus girls tucked around Romans 8:26 about weak places.

> There is now no condemnation for those who are in Christ Jesus.
> ROMANS 8:1

> You, however, are not in the realm of the flesh but are in the realm of the Spirit.
> ROMANS 8:9A

> If God is for us, who can be against us?
> ROMANS 8:31B

> No, in all these things we are more than conquerors through him who loved us.
> ROMANS 8:37

Maybe we need to sit still for just a moment or two today. Quietly sit without the weight of condemnation or the swirl of trying to figure things out. Quiet, with nothing but the absolute assurance the Spirit helps us in our weakness.

He understands our weak places. He knows what to pray. There is a purpose to this weakness. Though it doesn't feel good, things will be worked out in a way that good will come from it (Rom. 8:28).

In that quiet stillness while the Spirit prays for us and we just simply soak in truth, there will be a flicker of light. A slight trickle of hope. A grace so unimaginable, we'll feel His power overshadowing our weakness.

Even the smallest drop of God's strength is more than enough to cover our frailties, our shortcomings, the places where we deem ourselves weak. So we'll reject that title. We aren't weak. We are dependent. Dependent on the only One powerful enough to help us. The only One sufficient enough to cover us in grace throughout the process.

Our relationships are not sufficient. Our circumstances are not sufficient. Our finances are not sufficient. Our willpower is not sufficient. Our confidence is not sufficient. But He is and has been and forever will be sufficient.

How does this resonate with you personally?

Not only does Jesus love you, not only did He send an ~~Advocate~~ to help you, He also prayed for you. Here are just some of His words from His prayer in John 17:

> My prayer is not for them alone. I pray also for those who will believe in me through their message, that all of them may be one, Father, just as you are in me and I am in you. May they also be in us so that the world may believe that you have sent me. I have given them the glory that you gave me, that they may be one as we are one—I in them and you in me—so that they may be brought to complete unity. Then the world will know that you sent me and have loved them even as you have loved me. Father, I want those you have given me to be with me where I am, and to see my glory, the glory you have given me because you loved me before the creation of the world. Righteous Father, though the world does not know you, I know you, and they know that you have sent me. I have made you known to them, and will continue to make you known in order that the love you have for me may be in them and that I myself may be in them.
>
> JOHN 17:20-26

So, wherever you may be today, know that Jesus cares for you, wants you to call upon the Advocate, and is lifting you up in prayer to the Father. I challenge you to focus on that today and be reminded that Jesus is for you.

DAY 4

SEVEN I AMS

Can you believe that this is our last day of study together? I'm praying you felt the Lord speak to you as you studied His Word over these weeks.

One thing I've found is that I sometimes need to go back to a truth I've learned multiple times before it sticks. I really think this will be worth it and help us remember what God taught us over our time together.

What I want you to do is go back to each week of the homework, look over what you underlined, starred, or wrote in your personal study time and write three things that stood out to you during each week of study.

WEEK 1: Bread of Life

WEEK 2: Light of the World

WEEK 3: Good Shepherd and Sheep Gate

WEEK 4: Resurrection and the Life and the Way, the Truth, and the Life

WEEK 5: True Vine

To say I'm thankful for all we've learned in this study is such an understatement. I've needed this time for the presence of God to be personalized and personified through Jesus and His I AM statements.

My soul feels less entangled around the source of my sorrow.

I so very much recognize that I never told you all the details of what I've been wrestling through and praying for. My life is normally such an open book. And to some extent it is. But I've had to rip some pages out of my open book to protect the people with whom my story intersects. It's still all a bit untidy and complicated.

I'm not completely healed yet. I don't have all the answers. There hasn't been a big change in my circumstances. But I've shifted. My outlook is different. My perspective is more grounded in truth. And I feel more assured than ever that our good God has a plan. I just have to keep remembering He is God and I am not. There's a glorious sweetness in writing from the middle of a struggle. Because in the end, this was never about finding my answer. It was about finding "I AM." ✈

Finding and receiving all that Jesus is has been and will continue to be the biggest comfort of all. I have found all the many ways that He cares for me, comforts me, protects me, provides for me, and has a good way illuminated and marked out for me leading to eternity.

Jesus is mighty, but He's also tender. He's as big as the universe, but He's also incredibly personal and so very close. He is the Savior of the world, and yet He's also the intimate lover of my soul. He is everything I need, yes. But He's also everything I want.

So, I walk from this place with a profound exhaled realization. I am going be okay. Actually better than okay.

Because this is now what I will declare over my life:

Jesus, You are the satisfaction for every deep longing in my heart.

When I'm hungry for quick fixes or starving for affection or craving lesser things, Jesus, You are my Bread of life.

When I'm confused and anxious and exhausted from all my fragile efforts incapable of fixing my struggles, Your light brings clarity. Your light chases away my darkness. Your light of hope dispels the shadows of hurt.

You are the Good Shepherd who will find me no matter how lost or off course I wander. You speak tenderly my name and whisper wisdom I need. And then You encamp at the gate of my heart. You are the Sheep Gate, always there during my coming and going, protecting and providing for me.

When I get afraid of the daunting things that feel impossibly dead to me I will not be consumed with anguish or grief. Jesus, You are my Resurrection and my Life.

You are the Way when there is no way. You are the Truth in my life that silences the lies that scream in deafening tones. You are Life, certain and secure.

You are the true Vine I cling to and receive from all that's needed to not just survive but to thrive. What I am facing today may be a delay or a distraction or even a devastation for a season, but it is not a final destination. For You, the Great I AM, will have the final say. You will write the final words to my story. And because they come from You—the source of all that is good and right and true—the words of my life will be glorious.

This was never about finding my answer. This was about finding You, the Great I AM.

* Finding I AM declaration can also be found on page 176 and as a free download, along with Scripture Memory Cards at www.LifeWay.com/FindingIAm.

OPTIONAL
READ JOHN 18–21.

Good questions to ask as you read are:
What does this passage teach me about God?

_____

_____

_____

_____

_____

_____

_____

_____

_____

_____

_____

What does this passage teach me about myself?

_____

_____

_____

_____

_____

_____

_____

_____

_____

_____

_____

What do I need to do as a result of reading this passage?

_____

_____

_____

_____

_____

_____

_____

_____

_____

_____

As you read John today, see which of these attributes of God are exemplified and write out any thoughts you have about them.

Compassionate	Good	Faithful	Holy	Patient	Wise
Generous	Loving	Just	True	All-Knowing	
All-Powerful	Eternal	Gracious	Merciful	Faithful	

_____

_____

_____

_____

_____

_____

_____

_____

_____

Video Session 6

WATCH VIDEO SESSION 6 AND RECORD YOUR NOTES BELOW.

Scripture in this video session: John 15 • John 13:10

John 15:
   Bread of Life
   Light of the World
  The Sheep Gate
  Resurrection
   Way truth & Life

John 15:2-3
John 15:1-2
   15:8
True Vine

15:3 You & I are true Vine
John: You are always clean
  John 13:

Video sessions available for purchase
at www.lifeway.com/findingIAM

VIDEO GROUP DISCUSSION QUESTIONS

After watching the video, discuss the following questions in your group.

1. How has a relationship helped to prune you in the past? Share without revealing anything that might hurt someone.

2. Pruning makes us look more like Jesus. How have you seen that in your own life or the life of someone you know?

3. The vine has different seasons—planting, pruning, growing, producing, and then the harvest of the fruit. What season do you feel like you are particularly in at this moment and why?

4. How does it speak to you that when the Gardner prunes you, He is very close to you instead of distant?

5. How do the words *dwell*, *abide*, and *remain* connect with you right now? How could you step back from the busyness and stress of life to connect and abide with Jesus as a regular part of your life?

6. As we wrap up our study, so much of the themes we discussed were around how Jesus wants to be the true satisfaction in your life. Do you have any last minute insights about that as we leave this place today?

Leader Guide

Thank you for leading a group through *Finding I AM*. Thank you for your willingness to share of yourself and help other women dig into God's Word. I hope that this Leader Guide helps you as you study together.

If you'd like some promotional tools to help tell the story of the study and to get women on board and in your group, please visit *lifeway.com/findingIAM* to find these helpful resources.

You will find Group Guide pages for each session throughout the study. The Group Guide pages include room for notes to respond to the video teaching as well as discussion questions that a group can talk through following the video.

In the back of this Bible study book, you will find Scripture memory cards. Encourage your group members to memorize the I AM statements during the time of study. Memorizing these simple phrases will help them to know Jesus better and internalize the truth that He satisfies our every longing.

THE BASIC OUTLINE OF EACH GROUP SESSION WILL BE:

1. Discuss your personal study time from the past week. This Leader Guide will point you to specific questions from the week to look back on and answer together with your group.

2. Watch the video and take notes on what you hear.

3. Discuss the group questions on the Group Guide page.

4. Pray and dismiss.

For a study like this, the ideal time for your group is one hour. If you can meet longer, great, but you probably need at least an hour in order to have both good discussion and time to watch the videos.

TIPS ON LEADING:

1. PRAY: As you prepare remember that prayer is essential. Set aside time each week to pray for the women in your group. Listen to their needs and struggles so you can bring them before the Lord.

2. GUIDE. Accept women where they are but also set expectations that motivate commitment. Be consistent and trustworthy. Encourage women to follow through on the study, attend the group sessions, and engage in the personal study throughout the week. Listen carefully, responsibly guide discussion, and keep confidences shared within the group. Be honest and vulnerable by sharing what God is teaching you through the study. Most women will follow your lead if you share in a vulnerable way.

3. CONNECT. Stay engaged with the women. Use social media, email groups, or a quick note in the mail to connect with the group and share prayer needs throughout the week.

TIPS ON ORGANIZING:

1. Talk to your pastor or minister of education. If you're leading this as a part of a local church, ask for their input, prayers, and support.

2. Secure your location. Think about the number of women you can accommodate in the designated location. Reserve any tables, chairs, or media equipment for the videos that you may need.

3. Provide resources. Order the Leader Kit and the needed number of Bible Study books. You might need to get a few extras for last minute additions.

4. Plan and Prepare. Become familiar with the study and make notes of what information you need to share with your particular group.

SESSION 1

Use the first session to build fellowship within your group. Familiarize yourself with the content of the study. Preview the study for the members, so they will know what is expected each week.

1. Be sure each woman has a copy of *Finding I AM*.

2. Invite the women to introduce and share something about themselves, as well as what drew them to this study.

3. Without looking anything up, have women share what they think are some of the I AM statements of Jesus. See if as a group you can get them all (again, no cheating!).

4. Questions to ask your group:

   a. *Did you get them all right? Did you miss any? Did you think something was an I AM statement that really wasn't?*

   b. *Why do you think Jesus even said these I AM statements—why did He need to explain Himself in this way?*

5. The women don't have to answer this out loud, but before you start the video for this week ask them to silently think of one or two deep cries of their heart. Ask: *What is causing you heartache lately? What is a need in your life that God may not be meeting in the way you want right now?* (Again, this is the first group meeting—your group might want to discuss this especially if you all know each other well—but if not, at least have them think about and write some thoughts down on the notes page. Having this information front and center in their heads will help prepare them for the video.)

6. Watch Video Session 1 and discuss the questions in the Group Guide (pg. 10).

7. Review any information from the About This Study page (pg. 6) that you think women may need to know.

8. Instruct the participants to complete Week 1 of their personal study this week and come ready to discuss it at the next group meeting.

9. Pray and dismiss.

For Sessions 2-6 consider beginning each week with an invitation to group members to share from their personal study by asking the first question below. After question a, the following questions are all drawn from the week of personal study.

1. Questions to ask your group:

   a. *What was the most meaningful moment for you this week? It may be a Bible verse, principle, revelation, new understanding, or conviction.*

   b. *In what way has the enemy been tempting you to satisfy physical and emotional needs and kept you from pursuing that zoe life we've been reading about? (Page 19)*

   c. *How have you seen God show up in a seemingly impossible situation in your life or in the life of someone you know? (Page 23)*

   d. *Has there been a time in your life where God clearly provided for you in a way that only He could? Share your experience with the group. (Page 28)*

   e. *What storms have you tried to face on your own? Battles you've tried to fight without turning to Jesus? What are your go to "tools" that you pull out when you get into this kind of situation? (Pages 33-34)*

   f. *How can you guard against the seemingly never ending to do list of what you think you should do as a "good Christian" and remind yourself that believing in Jesus is all you need? (Page 35)*

2. Ask if anyone is planning on, or has started, the optional 5th day of study of reading through the Gospel of John. Encourage women to stick with it if they can.

3. Watch Video Session 2 and discuss the questions in the Group Guide (Pg. 38).

4. Pray and dismiss.

SESSION 3

1. Questions to ask your group:

   a. In your personal study, you learned about some of the Jewish festivals. Was there anything that you learned about them that was new to you? If so, share it with the group.

   b. What kind of traditions do you hold dear in your family now or from your family growing up? (Page 44)

   c. What are some things that you've done this very day that required water or light?

   d. What wells do you think our culture tries to draw water from on a regular basis? (Page 47)

   e. Read 2 Corinthians 11:14 and make a mental note of how Satan disguises himself. How have you seen that play out in the world or in your own life lately? (Pages 55-56)

2. Watch Video Session 3 and discuss the questions in the Group Guide (pg. 66).

3. Pray and dismiss.

SESSION 4

1. Questions to ask your group:

   a. This week we studied sheep. On Day 1 we discussed characteristics of sheep. Which characteristic was one you didn't know about sheep? And how do these characteristics remind you of us?

   b. On Day 2 we discussed both keys and barriers to hearing God's voice. What did you think of the list? Are there any others you might add to the keys list? What about the barriers? (Pages 79-80)

   c. What do you think it means for us to "come in and go out, and find pasture"? (Page 84)

d. On Day 3 we learned about how shepherds cared for their sheep. How does that information comfort you today?

e. On Day 4 we discussed head knowledge vs. heart knowledge. How can you find ways to not only know more about Jesus in your head, but also in your heart?

2. Watch Video Session 4 and discuss the questions in the Group Guide (pg. 100).

3. Pray and dismiss.

SESSION 5

1. Questions to ask your group:

   a. This week we studied the raising of Lazarus. On Day 1, Lysa asked: Why do you think Jesus waited two extra days after hearing that Lazarus was ill before He traveled back to Bethany? (Page 109) Discuss with your group your answers and also if there is something you may be waiting on from the Lord that He hasn't answered just yet.

   b. On Day 2 we talked about ways to press through unanswered prayers. What are the three ways outlined? Which one resonated with you the most?

   c. On Day 3 we explored the I AM statement of Jesus: I AM the Way, the Truth, and the Life. On Page 123, Lysa asked you what was both comforting, and not so comforting about that particular statement. How did you answer that question?

   d. Ask the group what reflections they had after they completed the Day 4 Prophecy Fulfilled activity. (Page 128) Was anything new to you on this list? If so, share and discuss in your group.

2. Watch Video Session 5. Note, in this particular video there is a clear call to accept the gospel if you have not. Be sensitive to your group for this time and think about the best way to bring this up and discuss together, as well as take next steps with anyone who did make the decision.

3. Discuss the questions in the Group Guide (pg. 132).

4. Pray and dismiss.

1. This is your last week together with your group. Congratulate your group on sticking with this study and praise their efforts for getting into the Word of God together. Challenge them to teach/lead others—either through leading this study with another person or group or simply by sharing some of the truths they've learned with those in their sphere of influence.

2. Questions to ask your group:

    a. On Day 1, Lysa asked a series of questions. If the group feels comfortable, ask them to share some of their answers to the questions: *In what ways do you feel "not enough" today or this week? How have you tried to cover this up in your life by doing something? Did it work? Did it mask the feeling? If so, for how long? (Page 139)*

    b. *This week on Day 2 we talked about pruning and abiding. Did anything from that material stand out to you in a new way?*

    c. *On Day 3 we began to wrap up our time together and we looked at some of the final words of Jesus. How did you answer this question: Read John 15:12-27. Are these the type of final words you might expect to hear from Jesus? Why or why not? (Page 147)*

    d. *On Day 3 we talked about how Jesus is our Advocate. How did you answer the question after the activity on page 150?*

    e. *As you went back and reviewed the I AM statements—what were you reminded of? What do you think will stick with you the most as we end our time together?*

3. If you did the optional reading through the Gospel of John, share any insights you had with the group. And let the group know that if they didn't read through the Gospel of John as they went, perhaps that is a good next step to do now that the official study is over.

4. Watch Video Session 6 and discuss the questions in the Group Guide (pg. 158).

5. Pray and dismiss.

Greek Dictionary

Bios - Breath in your lungs or physical life. (Page 17)

Zoe - possessed with vitality looking to the fullness of life (Page 17). Life, both of physical (present) and of spiritual (particularly future) existence (Page 126).

Zeteo - to crave. (Page 20)

Chaser - lack, be without, become empty (Session 4 Video)

Ginōskō - to come to know, recognize, perceive. (Page 94)

Eido - to know, remember, or appreciate. (Page 94)

Embrimaomai - anger, outrage, and emotional indignation. (Page 112)

Kardia - heart. (Page 122)

Hodos - a way, road, journey. (Page 123)

Alétheia - truth, but not merely truth as spoken, truth of idea, reality, sincerity, straightforwardness. (Page 124)

Menó - to stay, abide, remain, wait. (Page 143)

Paraklétos - called to one's aid or (a) an advocate, intercessor, (b) a consoler, comforter, helper, (c) Paraclete. (Page 150)

Endnotes

WEEK 1:

1. William Arndt, Frederick W. Danker, and Walter Bauer, *A Greek-English Lexicon of the New Testament and Other Early Christian Literature* (Chicago: University of Chicago Press, 2000), 177; Gerhard Kittel, Gerhard Friedrich, and Geoffrey William Bromiley, *Theological Dictionary of the New Testament* (Grand Rapids, MI: W.B. Eerdmans, 1985), 290.

1. Strong's NT 2212; *http://biblehub.com/greek/2212.htm.*

2. "declaration." Dictionary.com. *Dictionary.com Unabridged.* Random House, Inc. *http://www.dictionary.com/browse/declaration* (accessed: November 1, 2016).

3. Colin G. Kruse, *The Gospel According to John: An Introduction and Commentary* (Grand Rapids: Wm. B. Eerdmans Publishing, 2003), 162-163.

4. Sinclair Ferguson, *The Whole Christ: Legalism, Antinomianism, and Gospel Assurance* (Wheaton, IL: Crossway, 2016), 47.

5. Dorothy K. Patterson and Rhonda H. Kelley, eds. *Study Bible for Women-HCSB,* (Nashville: B&H, 2015), 208.

6. Hayyin Schauss, *The Jewish Festivals: From Their Beginnings to Our Own Day* (New York: Union of American Hebrew Congregations, 1938), 46.

7. Michael Card, *John: The Gospel of Wisdom* (Downers Grove, IL: InterVarsity Press, 2014), 84.

WEEK 2:

1. Kevin Hall, "Jesus: The Light of the World," *Biblical Illustrator*, Winter 2013-2014.

2. Hayyim Schauss, *The Jewish Festivals: A Guide to Their History and Observance* (New York: Schocken, 1938),181.

3. Based on the illustration "Herod's Temple" by Bill Latta is taken from *Holman Illustrated Bible Dictionary*© 2003, B&H Publishing Group, pp. 1564-1565. Used by permission.

4. Strauss, 183.

5. Ibid.

6. Spurgeon, C. H. "The Light of the World." In *The Metropolitan Tabernacle Pulpit Sermons*, 62:501. (London: Passmore & Alabaster, 1916.)

7. Lyrics from John Newton's "Amazing Grace."

8. Kenneth W. Osbeck, *Amazing Grace: 366 Inspiring Hymn Stories for Daily Devotions* (Grand Rapids, MI: Kregel Publications, 1990), 164.

WEEK 3:

1. Warren Weirsbe, *Jesus in the Present Tense* (Colorado Springs: David C. Cook, 2011), 82.

2. Kruse, 232-234.

3. "Matthew 26:40-41," *Life Application NIV Bible* (Carol Stream, IL: Tyndale, 2001), 115.

4. Taken from Lysa TerKeurst, *Uninvited* and *Uninvited: A DVD Study* (Nashville: Thomas Nelson, 2016).

5. Beauford H. Bryant and Mark S. Krause, *John, The College Press NIV Commentary* (Joplin, MO: College Press Pub. Co., 1998), Jn 10:11.

6. Ibid.

7. Strong's NT 1097; *http://biblehub.com/greek/1097.htm*.

8. Strong's NT 1492; *http://biblehub.com/greek/1492.htm*

9. Paul J. Achtemeier, Harper & Row and Society of Biblical Literature, *Harper's Bible Dictionary* (San Francisco: Harper & Row, 1985), 938.

WEEK 4:

1. Clifton J. Allen, *Broadman Bible Commentary*, Vol. 9 (Nashville: B&H, 1969), 314.

2. Strong's NT 1690; *http://biblehub.com/greek/1690.htm*.

3. D. A. Carson, *The Gospel According to John, The Pillar New Testament Commentary* (Leicester, England; Grand Rapids, MI: Inter-Varsity Press; W.B. Eerdmans, 1991), 415.

4. Clay Ham and Mark Hahlen, *Minor Prophets, The College Press NIV Commentary* (Joplin, MO: College Press Pub. Co., 2001), 328.

5. Strong's NT 2588; *http://biblehub.com/greek/2588.htm*.

6. Strong's NT 3598; *http://biblehub.com/greek/3598.htm*.

7. Strong's NT 225; *http://biblehub.com/greek/225.htm*.

8. Strong's NT 2222; *http://biblehub.com/greek/2222.htm*.

WEEK 5:

1. Strong's NT 3306; *http://biblehub.com/greek/3306.htm*.

2. Warren Weirsbe, *He Walks with Me: Enjoying the Abiding Presence of God* (Colorado Springs: David C. Cook, 2011), ebook.

3. Strong's NT 3875; *http://biblehub.com/greek/3875.htm*.

Notes

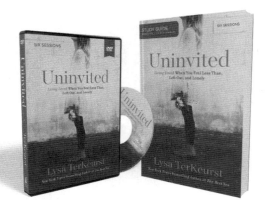

The free app you've been looking for!
Give God your first thoughts every day.

"We must exchange whispers with God before shouts with the world."
Lysa TerKeurst

We say we put God first... so wouldn't it make sense that we give Him the first 5 minutes of each day? That's why Proverbs 31 Ministries created the

· Honor God by letting His truth direct your first thoughts of the day and discover how much healthier your perspective of life becomes.
· Discover unique parts of the Bible you may have missed by studying one verse in one chapter, one day at a time.
· Replace feelings of comparison and rejection that social media often brings by starting your day with the truth of God's Word.
· Gain confidence in your ability to navigate Scripture by learning to identify the major moments in each chapter.

Download the app for FREE!

Download on the **App Store**

Get it on **Google play**

FIRST5.ORG

ABOUT PROVERBS 31 MINISTRIES

Lysa TerKeurst is the president of Proverbs 31 Ministries,
located in Charlotte, North Carolina.

If you were inspired by Finding I AM and desire to deepen your own personal
relationship with Jesus Christ, we have just what you're looking for.

Proverbs 31 Ministries exists to be a trusted friend who will take you by the
hand and walk by your side, leading you one step closer to the
heart of God through:

Free First 5 app
Free online daily devotions
Online Bible studies
Writer and speaker training
Daily radio programs
Books and resources

For more information about Proverbs 31 Ministries,
visit www.Proverbs31.org.

Connect with Lysa at www.LysaTerKeurst.com
or on social media @LysaTerKeurst.

We'll put the kettle on.

The kind of conversation you'd have over tea with your best friend. That's the LifeWay Women blog.

Drop by to grow in your faith, develop as a leader, and find encouragement as you go.

Find Bible studies, events, giveaways, and more at **LifeWayWomen.com**

Sign up for our weekly newsletter at *LifeWay.com/WomensNews*

LifeWay | Women

Jesus,

You are the satisfaction for every deep longing in my heart.

When I'm hungry for quick fixes or starving for affection or craving lesser things, Jesus, You are my *Bread of Life*.

When I'm confused and anxious and exhausted from all my fragile efforts incapable of fixing my struggles, *Your light* brings clarity. Your light chases away my darkness. Your light of hope dispels the shadows of hurt.

You are the Good Shepherd who will find me no matter how lost or off course I wander. You speak tenderly my name and whisper wisdom I need. And then You encamp at the gate of my heart. *You are the Sheep Gate,* always there during my coming and going, protecting and providing for me.

When I get afraid of the daunting things that feel impossibly dead to me I will not be consumed with anguish or grief. *Jesus, You are my Resurrection and my Life.*

You are the Way when there is no way. *You are the Truth* in my life that silences the lies that scream in deafening tones. *You are Life,* certain and secure.

You are the true Vine I cling to and receive from all that's needed to not just survive but to thrive. What I am facing today may be a delay or a distraction or even a devastation for a season but it is not a final destination. For you, the Great I AM, will have the final say.

You will write the final words to my story. And because they come from You—the source of all that is good and right and true—the words of my life will be glorious.

This was never about finding my answer.
This was about finding You, the *Great I AM.*

#FINDINGIAM

I AM THE

Bread of life.

JOHN 6:35

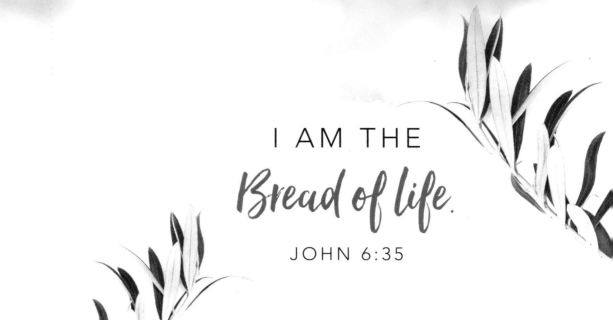

I AM THE

Light of the world.

JOHN 8:12

I AM THE *Gate.*

JOHN 10:9

I AM THE

Good Shepherd.

JOHN 10:11

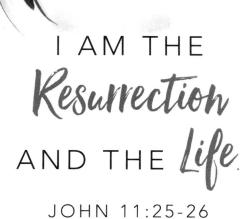

I AM THE

Resurrection

AND THE *Life.*

JOHN 11:25-26

I AM THE *Way*

AND THE *Truth*

AND THE *Life.*

JOHN 14:6

I AM THE TRUE *Vine.*

JOHN 15:1

I AM THE *Bread* OF LIFE. JOHN 6:35

I AM THE *Light* OF THE WORLD. JOHN 8:12

I AM THE *Gate.* JOHN 10:9

I AM THE *Good Shepherd.* JOHN 10:11

I AM THE *Resurrection* AND THE *Life.* JOHN 11:25-26

I AM THE *Way* AND THE *Truth* AND THE *Life.* JOHN 14:6

I AM THE TRUE *Vine.* JOHN 15:1